FOR THE LOVE OF DARLO

FOR THE LOVE OF DARLO

My Life and Fifty Years Supporting Darlington FC

PAUL HODGSON

pitch

First published by Pitch Publishing, 2024

Pitch Publishing
9 Donnington Park,
85 Birdham Road,
Chichester,
West Sussex,
PO20 7AJ
www.pitchpublishing.co.uk
info@pitchpublishing.co.uk

A CIP catalogue record is available for this book from the British Library.

ISBN 978 1 80150 744 8

Typesetting and origination by Pitch Publishing

Printed and bound in India by Thomson Press.

Contents

For my wife, Jennifer, who is my soulmate and best friend.

Foreword

I FIRST became aware of Paul's incredible story in 2014 when I was approached by a member of the team producing the film based on his life, *Give Them Wings*. Having been invited to come on board the project to play Paul's love interest, Jane, and on learning more of the amazing efforts being made by Paul and the whole team to raise funds, I knew this was something I wanted to be a part of.

Despite many setbacks and a serious car accident, Paul continued to steadfastly coordinate the raising of funds during the following years. He showed determination and strength of character throughout and never lost sight of the goal he had set himself. In the latter part of 2019 all of this hard work, combined with the amazing efforts of the whole production team, came to fruition and filming finally began.

I am immensely proud to say that the finished film fulfilled my expectations, not only reflecting Paul's triumph over adversity but also as an inspiration to others showing what can be achieved by dedication, determination and the value of good friends.

It just remains for me to wish Paul the very best for the future and with this, his latest book.

Katie Sheridan
Actress

Acknowledgements

THANKS TO my wife Jennifer for her never-ending patience, and my PA Chris for his constant practical help. I'd also like to say a massive thank you to all my friends for their support along the way, especially Ian Carter, Stephen Lowson and John Gray – all of whom feature in this book. In addition, I'd like to thank the following ex-Darlington players who through playing for the club have become firm friends: Mark Forster, Kevan Smith, Roger Wicks and Michael Smith.

Also, many thanks to my school friend Rob Punton for reminding me of many stories that I'd forgotten about, and for sending me his diary which included many instances that were of use to me. I'm extremely grateful to him for allowing me to include them in this book.

Finally, special thanks to my friend and actress Katie Sheridan who kindly wrote the foreword for this book. I'm extremely grateful to her for this.

Introduction

WHEN I wrote *Flipper's Side* in 2000 and *Give Them Wings* in 2021, I didn't feel ready to go into great detail about my school days.

After a long discussion with Jennifer and after she'd heard what had happened to me at both Salters Lane School in Darlington and Percy Hedley School in Newcastle, her first words were, 'There is another book in there, Paul.' I thought about it and then replied, 'You could be right there Jen.'

As I have mentioned throughout this book, I've been honest. The facts are true; however, some of the conversations may not be word-for-word correct. I have to stress that this takes nothing away from the honesty I've displayed throughout this story.

I have to say, recalling some of the incidents was difficult, but I was 100 per cent determined not to leave anything out, otherwise I would have been defeating the whole object of writing it.

The story has a mixture of funny and indeed not so amusing tales. I really hope that you enjoy reading it.

Paul Hodgson

Chapter 1

MY NAME is Paul Hodgson. I was born on 7 March 1965 to Norman and Alice Hodgson in Darlington, County Durham. Interestingly now, I was a perfectly healthy baby boy when I was born.

However, my parents' lives were shattered when I was taken seriously ill at only seven months old. After examining me, our family doctor reassured my mother, telling her not to worry.

This is how my mother remembered the build-up to what happened in late 1965. It goes without saying that she received the earlier information from my father. It may not be 100 per cent factually correct. However, the piece regarding my illness certainly is.

One lunchtime, my father wheeled his bicycle over the cobbles. As he reached the back door to our house, he pushed at the rickety gate, which eventually opened.

He appeared at the back door and my mother looked disapprovingly at his muddy boots and said, 'Don't you even think of coming in here with them on. I've just finished scrubbing the floor.' He put down the basket and bent down to remove his boots.

Anyway, a few minutes later, my father sat down at the table and asked, 'How long is dinner going to be?' My mother replied, 'It's ready.' In the meantime, I was crying in the background. My mother ladled stew while my father washed his hands at the kitchen sink. She then said, 'That's our Paul again. He's hardly slept a wink.' My father ignored the comment as he tucked into his stew.

Finally, after eating two bowls of the stew, my father looked at my mother and asked, 'What did the doctor say is up with our Paul, then?' By this time my mother was cradling me. She replied by revealing, 'He thought he might just be teething and that he might have a bit of a cold, but I told him there's no sign of any teeth coming through yet and to me it looks far more than a cold. Also, I think he's got a rash coming now. What do you reckon?' She then lifted up my clothing for my father to see. He gave the rash a quick glance before stating, 'Look, the doctor said not to worry, so don't. I'm sure he'll be right as rain tomorrow.' Alice glared at him before saying, 'There's more to this than any flaming cold, that's for sure. I'm not stupid.'

Norman then put his boots on followed by his Darlington hat and scarf. My mother looked at him and asked, 'Who are Darlington playing today?' He replied, 'Wrexham. I'll see you later.' With that, without uttering another word, he got up and left the room, leaving my worried mother with a very sick baby in her arms.

Half an hour later, Norman was at the turnstiles at Darlington Football Club. All he could hear was the programme seller shouting, 'Programmes! Come and get your programme here! Only four pence!' As per his routine, he queued up and bought a copy, before heading into the ground.

At almost exactly the same time, Alice brought me a bottle. As she got close to my cot, she noticed something unusual. My face contorted. She paused for a few seconds, not quite believing what she was seeing before looking on in sheer horror and screaming, 'Paul!' She then panicked and rushed out of the room.

A few seconds later, she returned with a neighbour who asked, 'What's this all about Alice? Calm down, just calm down.' My mother by this time was crying uncontrollably. In between the tears, she spluttered out, 'Our Paul's just had a fit. Oh, God, please don't let him die. Please don't let him die!' The neighbour then ran outside and caught the attention of a young boy who was playing football in the street and told him to run to the phone box and ring 999 to get an ambulance. The boy nodded, left his football outside our front door and sprinted down the street towards the phone box.

The neighbour then said to my mother, 'Right, Alice, come with me.' With that, and my mother still cradling me, they went into my parents' bedroom where my neighbour quickly stuffed some clothes into a bag.

Ten minutes later, in the distance the clanging of an ambulance could be heard.

Meanwhile, my father was watching the football, blissfully unaware of what was unfolding at home. All of a sudden, a tannoy announcement blasted around the ground. It said, 'This is an urgent message for Norman Hodgson. Please go to the office immediately.' My father's head was buried in his programme. A supporter tapped him insistently on the shoulder before saying, ''Ere. That's you, Norman.' Norman reacted by barging past the fans in front of him and headed straight to the office, where he was given the news that I'd been rushed into hospital.

On arrival at the hospital, Norman ran towards Alice, almost colliding with a patient who was being wheeled along on a stretcher by an orderly. My sobbing mother held on to him while he caught his breath. Alice cried, 'It's our Paul.' Norman looked at her and then enquired, 'Is he going to be all right?' Alice shrugged her shoulders before revealing, 'I don't know. They've put all sorts of tubes in him. He's in there.' They both peered through the round glass panel of a door. Two doctors and a nurse were bent over me as I was in a cot.

A few days later, my parents were sitting at the specialist's desk eager to hear what was wrong with me.

This is what my mother told me happened that day. Again, the following is not word-for-word factual; however, the story certainly is.

The specialist started by stating, 'Mr and Mrs Hodgson, I've been treating Paul. He's really poorly and after running some tests, we've ascertained that he's contracted meningococcal meningitis.' My father gave him a questioning look and asked, 'Meningococcal meningitis? What's that?' The specialist replied, 'It's an inflammation of the brain and spinal cord. I must warn you that it's not looking good.' My mother responded by asking, 'What does it mean for Paul?' The specialist shook his head, paused for a few seconds, seemingly not quite sure how to word his next sentence, and then answered by revealing, 'I'm going to be honest with you, Mrs Hodgson. If Paul survives, and I mean IF, he'll suffer brain damage and will never walk. Communication will be extremely difficult, In other words, he will need a lot of care for the rest of his life.'

Alice started to sob and Norman awkwardly tried to comfort her by putting his arm around her shoulder. The specialist continued by saying, 'In the event that Paul does survive, we will be able to see what we can achieve with regard to improving his overall situation. But I can't stress enough that the next few weeks will be critical.' Alice nodded. The specialist went on to explain, 'We can only wait and see as Paul grows and develops what effect this will have on his body. What you both need to think about is whether you are strong enough to cope with a severely disabled child or whether you'd need to place him into care.' My mother vehemently shook her head as tears flowed down her cheeks. After composing herself, she responded by saying, 'That won't happen while I'm around, doctor.' Norman simply remained quiet.

Chapter 2

DURING MY early years, not only did I have great difficulty in making myself understood, I was so uncoordinated that I had to be propped up against a wall with cushions, like Christy Brown in that brilliant film *My Left Foot*. Although I do have some movement in my legs, from the age of four I've been a wheelchair user.

For someone with special educational needs like me, it was therefore vital that I was given every opportunity to make the most of my limited physical abilities and shine academically.

Luckily, my first real taste of education was at the fairly enlightened Salters Lane Special School in Darlington.

I can remember being on the bus going to school on my very first day when we stopped at some traffic lights. A group of Teddy Boys took great delight in picking up some mud and hurling it at the bus windows before shouting 'Spackers'. It was certainly a scary experience, one that I never forgot. In fact, despite being very young, it stuck in my mind for many, many months afterwards.

CHAPTER 2

For some strange reason, at first I was put in the school up the road from Salters Lane which was called Mayfair and was for children with severe learning difficulties. Even at such a young age, I can remember thinking, 'Why am I here? This place doesn't feel right for me,' or words to that effect. In other words, I knew that I wasn't in the right place.

I was correct and my mother was quite rightly absolutely appalled and wrote to my consultant, Dr Markum, who went on to write a very strongly worded letter to the council's education department and within two days I was transferred to Salters Lane School. Though looking back at my very short time at Mayfair School, it was a tad scary being there. I can remember some members of staff restraining the kids and indeed yelling at them, which certainly wouldn't happen in today's society. Fortunately, they liked me, probably because I didn't give them any problems. Several of them said to my mother that I shouldn't have been put there in the first place. As I mentioned, she already knew that anyway.

Prior to me telling you about my time at Salters Lane School, I thought I'd give you a brief history of the place.

The school was built in 1929 and catered solely for physically disabled youngsters between the ages of four and 16. It was also commonly known as the 'Open Air School'. Interestingly, the reason for this was because in the past, it had exposed its so-called 'delicate' pupils, who were suffering from breathing disorders such as asthma or chronic bronchitis, to a regime of outdoor exercise, fresh air and sunlight. It was thought that this strict regime would be of great benefit to their health.

I entered the newly opened nursery unit of the school in 1969 when I was only four years old. I can remember thinking, 'What a difference this is from the other place. The kids aren't being shouted at every few minutes.' I have to say, after being in that environment, this new place was like heaven to me.

Anyway, one of my very first lessons springs to mind. Let me recall it for you.

I was sitting in a circle of children around a teacher called Mrs Barnfather. She had a wooden dummy clock in her lap (I can remember thinking at the time that it was huge) and was moving its massive hands around in an attempt to show us how to tell the time.

At this stage of my tale, I must inform you that I had already been taught how to tell the time by my father when I was only two and a half years old. I have to say that looking back, it was probably one of the few good things that he ever did for me during my whole life until the day he passed away in 2019. Even he was amazed by how fast I picked it up. Much later, my mother told me that he'd commented on it at the time. Maybe he was proud? I don't know. I'd like to think he was though.

So, returning to the lesson, despite my really bad speech impediment, when it was my turn I confidently proclaimed, 'Two o'clock,' to which Mrs Barnfather replied, 'Good guess, Paul.' Clearly, she didn't honestly believe that a boy of four could know the answer without having received prior instruction from her. Even at such a young age, I knew that this simply wasn't the case.

Seeking further proof of my precocious ability, the teacher altered the hands of the clock and asked me again. I said, 'Five o'clock.' This time Mrs Barnfather proclaimed that I was 'lucky'. But when she pointed at the clock on the classroom wall and I gave the correct answer yet again, she rushed to fetch Mr Smith, the headmaster. In his presence, Mrs Barnfather set the clock to a different time and asked, 'What time does the clock say now, Paul?' I proudly announced, 'Twenty-five to nine.' This was the fourth time that I'd given the correct time. My mother told me that Mr Smith had written to her proclaiming that I could tell the time. She replied stating that she already knew and that I'd been able to for the past 18 months. I'm not sure whether Mr Smith believed her, but I knew it to be true.

So, as you can see, I was a very bright little boy for my age. I could even read a thermometer (I can remember one winter's morning, it was particularly cold and I glanced at the thermometer and said it was four degrees in the classroom. Mrs Barnfather was again amazed and gave me a 'double take', but was quite rightly more interested in getting the heating switched on) as well as being able to tell the time. Interestingly, that day, the heating never did come on, and all the pupils were sent home. I can remember going to my aunt's house next door to us as my mother and father were at work. I recall that she let me play with my cousin's toy soldiers, which I enjoyed. I can, however, remember that he wasn't keen on me playing with his toys. I often wonder if he ever found out. When my mother came to take me home, I can recall my aunty hurriedly picking the toy soldiers up, putting them back in their tin and putting them back in the cupboard. So I guess that he was none the wiser!

Anyway, returning to Salters Lane School, and on those cold mornings, I can remember being given a huge cup of hot chocolate. In theory, this was a good idea, as it would warm me up. The only problem was that the cup was too big and indeed too heavy (it resembled the size of a bucket and for a little boy like me, it weighed a ton) and therefore totally impossible for me to lift. Unfortunately, there weren't enough staff to assist me, as well as all the other children who needed help with this task. I should point out that this was well before the time that teaching assistants were brought in, so the drink just got left, which was a shame as I would have loved to have had it. I did try to pick the cup up on several occasions, but as I mentioned earlier, it was simply too heavy and without a doubt, the contents would probably have ended up down my clothes and scalded me in the process. I should add that several of the other children had the same problem as me. Looking back now, you'd have thought they would have changed the cup size to a smaller one or given me a straw, but they never did. The result was that more than half of the hot chocolate was wasted every day!

At around that time, another teacher called Mr Gafney taught me how to use an electronic typewriter. I remember vividly that it was a huge, bulky IBM machine, which came in very handy because by the time I was five years old, I knew where all the keys were on a keyboard. Mr Gafney was surprised that I picked up the basics of typing so quickly.

Unfortunately, despite having ever-improving mental faculties, these were undermined by a lack of bodily control. I can recall, for example, with some embarrassment, being dropped off at home by the school minibus. When Mrs Caton, the carer, pushed my wheelchair to our front door, she would hand my mother a small bundle and whisper, under her breath, 'There's your parcel, Mrs Hodgson.' Inside was a pair of my soiled underpants, because I was frequently incontinent at the age of five. With this in mind, I would have a supply of clean underclothes at the school so that I could be changed. Speaking of Mrs Caton, I really liked her and even after I left Salters Lane, I visited her at her house on a regular basis until she died many years ago.

As I mentioned above, by the age of five I knew all the letters on its keyboard off by heart and was typing simple stories, much to Mr Gafney's delight. At around that time my mother received a letter from Mr Smith stating that I was way ahead with my education, which pleased her very much.

As a matter of interest, by the time I was five, I also knew the alphabet off by heart and could do up to my six times table. Not bad for someone of that age, even if I say it myself!

Returning to Mr Gafney, he took a great interest in me and often took me swimming in his own time. I recall vividly him being armed with a huge rubber ring which he placed me into, in order that I could float in the water. On reflection, as I think back while writing this I can honestly say that we spent many happy hours at Darlington swimming baths. He reminded me of Mr O'Dowd, whom I met at Percy Hedley School and I shall talk about in great detail in a later chapter. Interestingly, I never did learn to swim, but looking back, it didn't really matter as I certainly had great fun, which was all that mattered to me at the time.

One other thing I loved doing at Salters Lane was pony riding. I was held on to the pony by two assistants (who as far as I know were trained volunteers) and was taken around the school field. The pony I was led around on was called Cornflake. The beasts were brought in from a local riding school and the handlers were really patient with the kids. In fairness, the animals were too. I can honestly say that the pony riding was my lasting memory from that school. I absolutely loved it and eagerly looked forward to it from the day the ponies were put back into their horseboxes and taken back to the training centre until the day they returned, two weeks later.

Chapter 3

HOME AT that time was a two-bedroomed terraced house in Dundee Street, Darlington, which in 1979 was extended so that I had a downstairs walk-in shower. When I was a little boy I had to be carried upstairs by my mother (for some reason, my father never seemed to be around at that particular time) for a bath, which was extremely awkward to say the least, especially as I got older. I have to say, my mother did struggle, especially when I got to the age of 14 or 15; hence the urgent need for the extension. I can remember that my father wasn't keen because we didn't get a 100 per cent grant and he didn't want to pay the excess. However, my mother won that argument hands down and after a few rows, the money was eventually paid to the council. It wasn't that he didn't have the money; he simply didn't want to part with it. If it had been left to him, the house could fall down around his ears.

Much later, long after my mother and I left home and she had sadly passed away, this was actually the case. When he passed away himself, I was actually appalled at the conditions he'd been living in when

I visited his house for the first time in many, many years. Like I said, it isn't as though he didn't have the money to get general repairs done, because he did. He was simply too greedy, that unfortunately was the bottom line. Apart from a new roof, which he had no choice to get put on, as the whole house was leaking and therefore filling up with water, next to nothing else was repaired or replaced. My mother and I left him in 1989 and right up until he died, he had the same carpets and furniture that were there when we upped sticks. In my opinion, that says it all really. Looking back now, I find it both sad and indeed pathetic. If he'd had no money, then I could have understood it, but he did (probably the money that he kept and left my mother no choice other than to have two or three jobs in order to keep the house going – it didn't do him any good though because as I once predicted, he died a lonely old man).

Anyway, back to my story. Until I was seven I slept in the back bedroom. However, as I grew older and became much heavier, the downstairs front room became my bedroom. This meant that prior to getting the walk-in shower installed I only had to be carried upstairs every other day for a bath, rather than every night to go to bed. This made life much easier for my mother.

My family circumstances can be briefly recounted as follows: my mother's maiden name was Alice Wood and she was born in 1930 in Wakefield, West Yorkshire.

She was one of five children. Her mother died in 1942 when my mother was only 12. Alice later told me that her mother (Mary Ann Davison, 1901–1942) was ironing one day and burned her arm. She didn't get it seen to by a doctor, therefore it got badly infected and eventually, it killed her.

Interestingly, when my grandmother died, my grandfather (George William Wood, 1904–1973) was away fighting in the Second World War. With this in mind, all the kids were split up and were sent to stay with various other family members. My mother told me that she stayed with her grandparents (on her mother's side; Henry and Ada Davison, née Gott). Apparently they were really kind to her while she was there and considering the sad circumstances, she enjoyed the time that she spent with them.

Speaking of my grandfather, he died in 1973 when I was only eight years old. I can, however, remember really liking him very much. I can distinctly recall him sitting on the floor with me playing with my toy cars when my mother and I used to go visit him and his second wife (Lilian Rudd Harrison, 1902–1994). I can honestly say that I enjoyed spending time with him and I was really upset when he passed away.

One further comment about George William Wood. Much later in life I started taking a great interest in family history. Looking back, I wished that I had asked him about his time in the war. But I suppose an eight-year-old doesn't think about that. Even so, I still regret him dying so early in my life and not finding out more about him.

When I visited my grandfather, I always admired a money box of his that stood on my grandparents' mantelpiece. Before he passed away, he told my grandmother that he wanted me to have it when anything happened to him. She abided by his wishes and I'm extremely proud to say that it is still in my possession to this day, 50 years after his death.

Returning to my tale (again), and after my grandfather remarried, my mother informed me that she practically brought her five brothers and sisters up herself as his new wife wasn't very nice with her stepchildren at all. Yet many years later, she was always very kind to me. Maybe it was the pressure of being responsible for five children who weren't hers. I simply don't know the answer to that one.

Anyway, after my mother left Ings Road Secondary Modern School in 1944 she started work at the Public Benefit Shoe Shop in Wakefield, but she didn't stay there long due to the low pay and unsatisfactory working conditions (she told me that it was like a sweatshop; even when she went to the toilet, she was timed by the supervisor and if he thought she'd taken too long, money was deducted from her wages). After leaving there, she went to work at Holdsworth Mill, which was only about a mile from where she lived, and she remained there until she moved to Darlington (where her stepmother was from) in 1948. She told me that she enjoyed working there and she was really sad to leave. Much later, she also mentioned to me she wished she'd stayed in Wakefield!

On arrival in Darlington, she quickly found a job at Pease's Mill in the town centre until she got married in 1950 to a local man, and over the years she gave birth to six children.

My mother left her first husband in 1962 and the six children from that broken marriage were either fostered or ended up in local authority care. Looking back, I don't know how she could do that, as I certainly couldn't. She must have had her reasons though. She would never talk to me about it, which I found strange as she was always open and honest to me regarding other parts of her life. I do know that money was short. Maybe she couldn't cope and got to the end of her tether. Again, I really don't know, but what I do know is everyone has their limits and maybe she reached hers. I feel that it is unfair for me to judge her without knowing the full facts. Anyway, she set up home with my father in 1964 and a year later I was born, as was my twin sister, who I've chosen not to include in this book.

By comparison with my stepbrother and stepsisters, I was brought up in a fairly stable, though far from ideal, environment. It became clear to me as I grew older that my mother and father had serious marital problems. (Looking back, I often wonder whether she used my father to get out of her previous relationship, although again I'm just speculating and I'll never know now.) However, without doubt, there were huge problems with their relationship. Very often, bickering between the two of them would manifest into damaging rows. I can remember one day my father threw a red sauce bottle at my mother. She ducked and it made a huge hole in one of the cupboard doors, which he very quickly repaired the following day.

I honestly don't know the reasons for such arguments and I wouldn't like to speculate on whether my disability had a part to play. Again, I'll never know now. However, they weren't happy together at all. Thinking back while writing this, now, I often wonder why she stayed with him for so long. He was greedy and kept her short of money and very lazy where paid work was concerned. He would often take four to six weeks off sick (with a bad back) at a time. Eventually he lost his job because of this. Putting it simply, he didn't like work because as mentioned above, he was lazy and therefore used his back as an excuse. Yet, despite being severely disabled, I worked for almost 40 years until my retirement in 2018. With this in mind, his work-shy excuses don't wash with me at all. This may sound harsh, but it's true. My reasoning for this is because despite being off sick with a 'bad back', he could still dig his allotment and carry heavy baskets of pigeons. It was because of this that I was determined not to be like him and I think I achieved that goal, which I'm really pleased about.

Looking back, he wasn't very easy to live with at all. How I stuck it until I was 24 I don't know, but that's a story for another day.

Anyway when I was seven, my world was turned upside down when my parents (mostly my mother) took the decision to send me to boarding school. The circumstances surrounding that choice will be explained in the next chapter.

Chapter 4

JUST BEFORE I started at Percy Hedley School, I can remember overhearing from the back door my parents having a huge row in the backyard about me going there. To this day, I honestly don't know what made me go to the back door. Maybe it was instinct. I guess I'll never know now. Anyway, the argument went something like this. Being only seven years old, I can't remember the exact words used, so I've used what I wrote for our film *Give Them Wings*. But the argument did happen.

The first thing I heard was my father yelling, 'Face facts, woman. Only you can fathom a word he bloody well says.' This made my mother really angry and upset. She responded by screeching, 'That's just my point! Paul needs to go to another school; one that will suit his needs better than Salters Lane. I want him to have the best chance in life. I honestly think that sending him to Percy Hedley School will give him that chance.' After drawing breath, she continued, 'The staff at Salters Lane aren't stretching him enough. Mr Gafney is great with him but I know in my own mind that to reach his full potential, he needs to go to Percy Hedley School.' I can remember my dad getting angrier by the minute. He responded by shouting, 'You are talking utter rubbish, woman.' My mother shook her head vigorously and yelled, 'You don't understand at all, Norman. I might as well talk to the back gate as talk to you. I'm putting my foot down about this, Paul is going to Percy Hedley School and that's that. I'm not discussing it any further with you because it's pointless.' My father shook his head and said coldly, 'Honestly, I don't care either way. At least he won't be under my feet all the time if he's there.' Alice was horrified, but simply shook her head and didn't say another word.

Without my parents seeing, I pulled myself away from the back door. I was utterly dejected, as from that day I knew exactly what my dad thought of me. It was certainly a lot to take in for a seven-year-old boy and I never forgot it.

A few days after my parents' blazing row, I can remember trying to discuss football with my father.

He switched on our new Bush colour television hoping to catch the football results. Instead, he turned it on just in time to hear, 'Division Four. Bradford City seven, Darlington nil.' He shook his head before shouting, 'The useless shower of shite! They need to get rid of that manager Ralph Brand. He's only at the club from a Thursday. What use is that? Plus that useless chairman George Tait needs to pack in as well. He's sacked almost as many managers as we've had games.

He's a clown.' Following his tirade, he turned the television off in temper.

After a few seconds I tried to speak, but the words simply wouldn't come out. My father looked at me angrily and asked my mother, who was knitting, 'What's he babbling on about?' She stopped knitting and responded by replying, 'To be honest, I don't know. But perhaps if you listened better, you'd understand him more.' My father ignored the comment and just shook his head without saying a single word. I then somehow managed to blurt out the word 'football'. My mother smiled at me prior to asking, 'Do you want a football, son?' I shook my head vigorously. She paused for a few seconds and thought. Suddenly as if it were a flash of lightning, it registered. She looked at my father and revealed, 'I've got it. He wants to *go* to the football, don't you Paul?' I nodded excitedly. He looked at her disdainfully and stated, 'The football! Is he soft in the head? Why the hell would he want to go there? He wouldn't understand what was going on anyway.' My mother angrily responded by shouting, 'Don't be like that, Norman. Paul may never be able to walk, but he's a bright lad with a mind of his own. Aren't you, son?' Before I could say anything, my father butted in and said, 'Face facts, woman. As I said to you the other day, only you can fathom a word he bloody well says. No bugger else can.' He then shovelled several lumps of coal on to the fire prior to throwing the shovel back in the scuttle.

By this time, my mother was really wound up and said, 'How do you know? Maybe you could understand him better if you made an effort. But just like with going to work, or more often not going, you are too bloody lazy to bother. Lots of fathers take their sons to the football, so where's the harm in that?' My dad glared at her before shouting loudly, 'Well I'm not lots of fathers. I'm not taking him and that's that. It's my final word on the matter.' My face dropped with disappointment. Alive looked at me and revealed, 'Don't worry, love. I'll take you one day.' Norman shook his head and yelled, 'Over my dead body! You aren't taking him either.' My mother obviously couldn't believe what she was hearing and replied, 'Norman! Don't talk like that and one other thing, just so that you are in no doubt, if I want to take Paul to Feethams, I will and neither you nor anyone else will stop me.' He ignored the comment and shouted, 'I'm off to the club now. At least I don't have to listen to this nonsense there.' With that, he left the room and slammed the door behind him.

Later, when my father came in from the club, the conversation continued. This is the gist of what was said. My mother told me many years later.

She started by stating, 'I thought you'd be there 'til chucking-out time. You're on the sick again, we have next to no money coming in, apart from my wages and you piss it up the wall. That's very clever, isn't it? You really are a selfish sod.' My father looked at her angrily and replied, 'I only went out because you were bloody well nagging. You were getting on my nerves.' She glared at him and queried, 'So getting pissed when we have next to no money is the answer, is it? You'll be the first to moan when there's no food on the table come the end of the week. Just remember, when I'm feeding Paul and there isn't much left for you, it's your doing, not mine. I won't let him suffer because of your actions.' My father paused and then replied, 'I'm going back to work in a couple of weeks so I don't know what you are going on about. We'll be fine until then.' 'No, we won't. So, what are we supposed to live on in the meantime? Plus, you've been off that many times, they'll be getting rid of you soon. You really are a lazy good-for-nothing, an absolute waste of space.' She paused for breath and then continued, 'Well, why won't you take our Paul to the football? Given that you are doing very little apart from feeding your pigeons, sitting on your fat arse and getting pissed down the club, it's the very least you could do.'

My father froze for a few seconds and then glared at her prior to blurting out the following, 'Look, I've said my piece. I'm not taking him and that's that. I'm not discussing this any more. Do you hear me, woman?' My mother shook her head in disgust and revealed, 'You know what your problem is, Norman? You're ashamed of your own son. You ought to be damn well ashamed of yourself, rather than Paul. You really are a disgrace and that's all I've got to say on the matter.' Norman was stunned by those words and simply left the room. Alice, who was by now in tears, shook her head in both disbelief and anger.

Chapter 5

A FEW days after my parents' huge argument, I can remember my mother pushing me past the bustling market stalls in Darlington town centre. Apart from the stalls themselves, which sold everything from clothes to shoes to fresh fish, I could only see a forest of legs which obstructed my view. Getting sidetracked (again), back in the 1970s, Darlington's outdoor market was bustling with dozens and dozens of stalls. People used to come from all over the north-east to visit, simply because at that particular time, it was one of the best markets in the area. Today, however, it is down to five or six stalls. Thinking about this as I work on this book, I find this fact really sad but unfortunately, it is a sign of the times that we live in.

Anyway, returning to my story, I turned around to face my mother as she pushed me and asked her, 'Where are we going, mam?' She smiled and then responded by revealing, 'It's a surprise son, so be patient.'

Eventually, after what seemed like a lifetime, (though in reality, it was only a few minutes) the pair of us found ourselves outside Feethams, the former home of Darlington Football Club. I can remember hearing the turnstiles making a regular clicking sound and rattles crackling into life as a path opened up for us both.

Outside the main gate, my mother stopped and pulled from her bag a black and white scarf and a woollen hat which she had obviously knitted herself. I smiled, looked at her and asked, 'Are we going to the football?' By way of an answer, she simply wrapped the scarf around my neck and put the hat on my head. She then said, 'There. That should keep out the cold. Right, let's ask someone how we get you in here.' At this point, I was almost overcome by sheer excitement at the prospect of seeing my hometown football team play.

Once inside the ground, I was totally gobsmacked by an air horn honking, galvanising the fans to beat with their fists on the resonant fabric of the Tin Shed stand so that it became akin to a huge echoing drum which reverberated around the whole of the then almost 100-year-old stadium. The fans began chanting, 'Da, Da, Da, Da, Da, Da, Da, Da, Da, Dar-lo!' I can remember being exhilarated by the sights and sounds of the match and beaming at my mother, who returned my smile. Even at such an early age, I could see that being there with her on that day brought her as much pleasure as it did me.

Saturday, 6 January 1973 is a date etched in my memory to this day. The previous game we'd been hammered 7-0 away at Bradford City as I mentioned earlier. So what was the score against Southport? Yes, you've guessed it, another 7-0 defeat. To me, on that day, the score didn't matter. The fact that my mother took me to see Darlington play meant so much more on that occasion and remains so to this day.

One final comment about me going to the football: my mother took me to several games and over the years, several players including striker Colin Sinclair, defender Clive Nattress and goalkeeper Phil Owers started noticing me and came over to where we were standing and introduced themselves to me, much to my delight.

A few days after my trip to Feethams, I was slouched in my wheelchair outside the front door, supported by cushions and reading the Southport programme as my seven-year-old neighbour, whom we'll call Scott, helped me to turn the pages. All of a sudden Scott stopped turning the pages and remarked, 'My mam says you're going away to a special school in Newcastle.' I scrunched up my face in disgust as my mother emerged from inside the house and overheard the conversation. She smiled and then glanced at my friend and revealed, 'We've already been and had a look round, Scott. Haven't we, Paul? It's a lovely school, isn't it?' I shook my head vigorously and then bemoaned, 'I don't want to go there, mam.' My mother gave me a stern look before stating, 'You have to. They'll teach you how to talk properly and do things for yourself.' Scott smiled at her and commented, 'That'd be good. It is hard to know what he says most of the time. But if I listen hard enough I do understand what he is saying.' I turned my wheelchair around in an attempt to get away from the conversation, having heard more than enough for my liking. Alice followed me, as I moved around, paused and then said with an emotional voice, 'Look, Paul, one day I won't be here to look after you. That's why you have to be able to do as much for yourself as possible.' Despite the difficulties that followed after that day, I remembered those words until the day my mother sadly passed away in 1994 and I often wonder what would have happened to me if I hadn't gone down the path she set me away on. Who knows, and I don't think she did for sure either at the time we had that conversation. I'm certain that in her own mind she thought she was doing the right thing.

Chapter 6

SO THE day came when I was taken to school by train by a woman who worked for the education department. I can remember the day as if it were yesterday. Here's my recollection of that traumatic day, one when I certainly knew that in my own mind I didn't want to go to the new school.

At around 11am one Monday in early January 1973, I was sitting in my wheelchair on the northbound platform at Darlington station with my mother, who was standing next to me, when a middle-aged woman wearing a thick winter coat and gloves approached us. She smiled, and then glanced at my mother before asking, 'Hello. Are you Mrs Hodgson?' My mother nodded and then returned the woman's smile and queried, 'That's right. You must be Paul's escort from the education department who is taking him to school?' The woman nodded and then responded by stating, 'Yes, I am. My name's Agnes. I'll make sure that Paul gets to school safely.'

Agnes held up a bag of sweets before asking my mother, 'Is it all right if Paul has these?' Alice nodded and then Agnes placed the bag of sweets on my knee. However, I had no intention whatsoever of accepting them and allowed them to drop on to the ground on purpose. I can remember they dropped with quite a 'bang'. I then glared at Agnes before announcing, 'I don't want any sweets!' My mother picked them up and handed them back to my carer for the journey prior to suggesting, 'If I were you, I'd give him them on the train, he's too upset at the moment.' Agnes nodded and then put them into her coat pocket. Alice looked at me and commented, 'That wasn't very nice letting them drop like that, Paul.' I simply put my head down, knowing in my own mind that I'd been rude. Thinking about it now, even at such a young age, I had decent manners. I have to admit that I let myself down that morning, and my mother quite correctly, but politely, pointed that out to me.

Shortly afterwards, the PA announcer let us know that my train was approaching the station by stating, 'The train approaching platform four is the 11.57 service to Newcastle, calling at Durham and Newcastle.' Agnes looked at me before confirming, 'Right, Paul. That's our train. You need to say goodbye to your mother now.' I can remember bursting into tears on hearing that piece of news. I was devastated. Alice bent down to my level, kissed my cheek and said, 'Now, be a good boy Paul and when you come back home, we'll go to the football again; just you and me.' She then half-smiled and continued, 'Hopefully, they will win next time!' Despite being bitterly upset with leaving her, I still managed to smile at that comment.

Just then a porter brought a ramp in order to get me on the train. After it had stopped, he opened the train door and set the ramp down and pushed me up it and into the carriage.

As the train pulled away, I can remember looking out of the train window and seeing my mother wiping her eyes with a handkerchief while she walked away from the platform. I never forgot that sight. At the time, I thought, 'How can she be so upset and still let me leave her at such a young age?' Obviously, I know the reasons now, but I couldn't get my head around it at that particular time.

Much later, one night when we were chatting, my mother told me that on the morning she took me to the station to set me off on my journey to Percy Hedley School, she came within an inch of changing her mind and sending me back to Salters Lane School instead. However, something stopped her at the very last minute. This is what she told me made her stick with her original decision, 'For purely selfish reasons, I could have kept you at home and continued to send you to Salters Lane School. But deep down, I had to think of you and what was best for you. I'd seen Percy Hedley School and I knew that the staff there would make my son as independent as he possibly can be and that is what I wanted for you, as I knew that I wouldn't be here for ever. So, although I didn't want to send you away, I knew that I was giving you the best chance in life by doing so.' These weren't her exact words, but the gist of what she told me.

After hearing what my mother said, I wondered what my life would have been like if I'd continued to go to Salters Lane School, rather than Percy Hedley. Would I have got as physically independent as I did? Would I have achieved what I have in my life? Being brutally honest, I don't know for sure. One thing I do know, despite having problems along the way during my time at Percy Hedley School, which I'll tell you about in the following chapters, I am of the opinion that my mother made totally the correct decision and shouldn't have felt guilty about it. She obviously did as she told me that she didn't sleep properly for weeks after I was sent away.

One final comment regarding this point: according to my mother, my father slept soundly from the first night I wasn't at home. Thinking about it today, that tells me a hell of a lot. Maybe he simply didn't show others how he was feeling, but that certainly wasn't the impression he gave me throughout my life.

Chapter 7

BEFORE I tell you the tale of my time at Percy Hedley, let me enlighten you with regards to the history of the place as I really feel that doing this could help you understand why certain things happened to me, and indeed many other disabled children. This part of my story is a bit of a roller-coaster ride, so hold on!

Looking through the history books and the internet, as well as speaking to my friend and former pupil Rob in order to research this book, it quickly became apparent to me that it was only because of the passion, determination and fundraising of several parents of disabled children that the Percy Hedley Foundation was founded in 1953, as a special school for children with cerebral palsy.

It's hard to imagine, in today's world, a time when disabled children couldn't access education. In the 1950s, it was not expected that any more could be done for children with cerebral palsy beyond what was already being done, but the parents, quite correctly, made it their mission in life to help their children realise their full potential and live life to the full. Thinking about it, those pioneering parents should be applauded for what they did. On the other hand, as Rob has frequently mentioned to me, did they create a monster, one that sometime in the future would escape and wreak havoc? Let me attempt to explain. I have to admit, doing so certainly isn't easy. (I re-wrote this piece many times before I was happy with it. This in my opinion just shows how difficult it was.)

When the first school opened there were only 12 students, but as of 2023 they supported over 650 members and their families each week through residential care, education, and finally lifelong learning opportunities, which on the face of it is very commendable, I have to say.

However, by the time I was entering the school this group had grown into a huge charitable organisation which was raising millions of pounds from public donations, resembling a business more than a charity. I often wonder what the original band of parents would make of the creature their idea became. Some now actually refer to it as a monster, just as Rob did.

Thinking about it, I would have thought that they are turning in their graves now feeling ashamed and indeed embarrassed by the capitalist beast it has manifested into. The money-grabbers have simply ignored or have conveniently forgotten the school's original purpose. As an adult in 2024, I can honestly say that I find this utterly unforgivable.

When people with brain and body defects are born, I honestly think that they are born with impairments and only become disabled when they encounter society: the lack of ramps, accessible transport or disabled toilets, etc. I don't have cerebral palsy as I wasn't born with it. This is the reason that I'm diagnosed as having 'cerebral palsy symptoms'. Getting back to my original point, I am actually unsure whether I am referring to the charitable society or society on a wider scale. I don't agree with charity on a personal level and I certainly don't consider myself a charity case. So maybe I'm referring to both, I don't know. Plus like many other things in life and indeed this book, it is a discussion for another day, or maybe another book!

Let us not lose sight of the fact that in the time of which I am referring the Social Model was a far-off dream. The only model out there was the Medical Model.

The reality of the situation is that society, right up until the late 1990s, simply had no idea how to deal with or indeed work with disabled people. So in essence, they were more than happy, if not grateful, that charities such as the Spastics Society could take that burden off their hands, from their minds, in order that they didn't have to think about it any more. 'Out of sight, out of mind' is a phrase that sums this up perfectly. If this meant they needed to throw these organisations vast amounts of cash, like what happened with the Percy Hedley Foundation and indeed many others, then so be it. I doubt our fate rarely, if ever, entered their thoughts. I have to say that I find this absolutely disgusting and unforgivable.

Rob told me what happened to him as a child one day when we were chatting on the phone ten or 12 years ago (he has also mentioned it in his diary), which I think reflects these opinions really well.

He was brought up within the Catholic faith and he openly admitted there were many times when he was sat at the rear of a cold, damp church, listening to ancient priests (according to Rob they all seemed ancient to him back when he was a young boy) preaching from the pulpit about curing people like him, and much later, he saw huge parallels between the Church and the Spastics Society or indeed other such charities. Both were transfixed with the notion of recovery over discovery. Making the disabled into the people (they think) they *should* be rather than helping them explore the people they *could* be. So, put simply, if both the Catholic Church and charities (at that time) had their way, the disabled person in question wouldn't get a choice and therefore would have no opportunity to improve his or her lot.

One particular conversation the pair of us had much later really stuck me. That of the Catholic Jesuits who are said to have claimed, 'Give me the child for the first seven years, I'll give you the man.' With charities, at that particular time, the span of years may be different, but the principle remains exactly the same. Of course, the other difference between the Church and charity is that the charity does not discriminate over gender, be you girl, boy, woman or man. According to Rob, the charity will screw you over equally. Interesting thoughts indeed!

Getting back to myself, thinking about it, I sometimes mistakenly refer to myself as a child of my time. In truth I was not a child of my time. I was a child of somebody else's time. If I were to choose my own life path, I would have attended the same educational facility as my friends (many of whom I lost touch with when I went to Percy Hedley School through no fault of my own) and I would have spent all my days in the family home (even though as mentioned previously it wasn't always ideal) but I had no choice or control over that. Even if I'd stayed at Salters Lane, I would have still been separated from able-bodied children. Thinking about this today, that situation simply can't be right.

Historically, the disabled have faced horrors and terrors yet look for reference to it in any history books (as well as Rob's diary) and there will be little or nothing to be found (I certainly struggled to find very much online). From infant-impaired babies left to starve to death in their own filth in their cots in a Boston hospital in the early years of the 20th century to horrors done during Aktion 4 to disabled people by Nazi Germany. From housing us in institutions far from civilisation to denying us the basic human rights of intimacy and physical love. These atrocities go on and no one ever seemed to have batted an eyelid. His story or indeed her story such as these seem in my opinion to be like 'gravy stains on your top' easily sponged away and instantly forgotten, unlike the Holocaust. The question you need to ask yourselves is, 'What is the difference between Aktion 4 and the killing of the Jews or indeed any other race during the Second World War?' The answer is simple. 'None.' Yet the hundreds of thousands of disabled children and indeed adults who were also murdered, hardly gets a mention anywhere. This fact begs the following question: does this mean the lives of the other people murdered by the Nazis were more important than the disabled people who were also killed? It makes me wonder to this day whether people just after the war thought this. They'd never admit it though, would they?

You must remember when I entered Percy Hedley School in 1973, it was less than 30 years after the Nazis in Germany enacted the horrors of Aktion 4 where disabled people were poisoned, starved or put to death by gassing – and they called it 'mercy killing'! This is where the phrase 'Useless Eaters' was born; a phrase that can be still seen and heard in certain circles today, which is totally unforgivable.

Interestingly, in 2013, my friend Ian Carter and I brought out a short film titled *An Unfortunate Woman*, which covered this subject. It was based on the story of Kathleen Mumford, who killed her disabled son to prevent him from being put into an institution. It was very harrowing to shoot, I have to say. The film actually went on to win quite a few awards, and was shown at the Cannes Film Festival. This was a huge honour; however, not for the first time have I said while writing this book, 'It's a story for another day.'

The story of my young life may seem a cakewalk by comparison, but I still think it deserves telling. In my opinion, it mirrors millions who have survived 'special education'.

One thing I need to get clear, what follows (in places) are MY thoughts. It is not meant as a judgement on 'special education'.

Chapter 8

ON ENTERING the doors at Percy Hedley School, it was at that very moment that I realised I was different from the other children in my street who went instead to the local schools and when it was time for me to leave home, as mentioned previously, I really did not want to go. Even though I was lucky in that I had a really good 'housemother' at Percy Hedley School called Elsie Ferguson, the transition from my home life in Darlington to the alien environment of the special school in Newcastle was hard to come to terms with, especially at such a young age.

Until I moved to Percy Hedley School, my mother had done virtually everything for me, and looking back today that was a huge mistake on her part. She realised that later, but at that time she still used to dress and feed me. This didn't do me any favours as I found out on my first full day as I was totally unprepared for what was about to be thrust upon me. Let me explain.

On my very first morning at my new school, I was bent over a washbasin, splashing my face with water. After I had finished, Elsie handed me a towel to dry myself, which I managed to do, albeit with difficulty.

To my horror, she then handed me a jumper for me to put on. I simply stared at it. Elsie then said, 'It won't put itself on, Paul. Put your arms in first and then lift it over your head.' I struggled to even get my arms in, so eventually, after seeing that I was getting nowhere fast, she gave me a hand. Once she'd got the jumper on me, she concluded by stating, 'Right, Paul, after breakfast, you're going to see Miss Carlisle in the gym.' I have to admit that as I left the bathroom, I couldn't help wondering what torture that particular event would have in store for me!

My first physiotherapy session with Miss Carlisle was extremely difficult to put it mildly.

Firstly, she lifted me out of my wheelchair, sat me on a foam mat and attempted to show me how to balance by sitting cross-legged. However, that for me wasn't as easy as you'd think, as when I tried to do it myself I was very unsteady and promptly fell over backwards and banged my head in the process. The pair of us tried this several other times. On each occasion, the result was exactly the same. I ended up on my back, unable to get myself up again. I suppose that I was a bit like a tortoise if you put it on its back. That can't move either!

From the physiotherapy session, I was taken to speech therapy. My therapist was Miss Birrell, and I'm still in touch with her today. She was one of my favourite members of staff and helped me greatly. I shall speak of her in a lot more detail later in this book.

Finally, after what seemed like an age, I spent time in my classroom. Once in there, I quickly noticed that there were a dozen pupils in my group which was made up of on average three wheelchair users, two or three who used walking aids and the remaining half a dozen or so were fully ambulant kids who had mild learning difficulties or behavioural issues. Interestingly, at that particular time, if a mainstream school within the catchment area felt even a little uncomfortable about accommodating such kids (which in most cases they should have), they would simply ship them in our school's direction and to other such schools across the country. Doing this made those children someone else's problem, rather than theirs. 'Out of sight, out of mind' came into play once again; I think that sentence sums this up perfectly. This scenario simply wasn't right in my opinion, both for the kids in question, and also the ones like my friend Rob and I who were quite clever.

The above situation resulted in a massive difference between learning skills and indeed learning speeds. This meant that no one in the class was adequately supported or educated, which for me and Rob in particular, was disappointing. Remember, as I mentioned earlier (the hot chocolate tale which happened on a daily basis at Salters Lane School), there were no such things as teaching assistants in those days. Looking back, this was certainly a huge disadvantage for me personally.

An amusing thing (in some ways) happened on my first day and indeed every other day. I quickly noticed that when the school bell rang the care staff disappeared like hot-blooded creatures hibernating during the winter season. If you blinked, you'd miss them! It was almost some sick magic trick. One minute they were there, the next, whoosh! And then they were nowhere to be seen. (Once again, thanks to Rob for reminding me of this.) It was unreal and thinking about it logically, it was a great pity that they didn't move that fast during lessons, as maybe fewer children would have messed themselves and ended up missing half a lesson while they were being cleaned up. An example of this is that one day a young girl needed to go to the toilet. She informed the teacher who in turn rang the person responsible for care that day.

That member of staff, despite two or three phone calls, took 35 minutes to come to the classroom, by which time the girl had messed herself. The carer was about to tell her off when the teacher pointed out that the girl in question had waited over half an hour and therefore it wasn't her fault. The carer simply put her head down. Later it was mentioned that the carer was finishing a cup of coffee but I don't know that for sure. However, I did notice that after that incident, that particular carer responded to the calls from the teacher much quicker!

I have to say, with the care staff doing their disappearing trick once the lunch bell rang, this meant that as a boy with fairly high support needs I had two options (not choices): either wet my pants or persuade one of my more able peers to support me to take a leak. Luckily, like Rob, I had some thoughtful, helpful friends. If you were charitable, I suppose you could say those were early lessons in independence training!

As an aside, like many other children, I noticed on my first day that the makeup of the school consisted of two elements: those pupils who attended daily, as they lived within travelling distance of the school, and those whose families and homes lived further afield. The catchment area of the school covered at least four counties: Northumbria, Cumbria, Teesside, and parts of North Yorkshire.

My father would pick me up most Friday afternoons (I stayed the odd weekend) and drop me off on the Sunday night.

Later, when more pupils from Darlington started to attend the school, and other schools in the South Tyneside area, a taxi was provided by the local authority to ferry us across.

You must be aware that this was years before accessible transport became a reality (ramped coaches, etc.). As a nine-year-old that would not have proven a problem; however, as a 15- or 16-year-old that was a completely different kettle of fish. The strain on both those being lifted and those doing the lifting must have been immense, as what happened with Rob. Luckily, I was taken home in a taxi, so it wasn't as bad for me.

Much later, we accidentally discovered that the taxi was active long before the school informed my parents, which meant they endured the financial strain for longer than was necessary. Another mark against the school pencilled into my mental notes! According to Rob, exactly the same thing happened to his parents.

Anyway, back to my story. Lastly on my first day, I went for 'feeding practice' with Elsie. A dinner lady brought over a steaming hot plate of dinner which she placed in front of me. I simply stared at it, expecting to be fed the food by Elsie. She looked at me and said, 'You not hungry, Paul? Come on, pick up your fork.' After several attempts, I eventually grasped the fork in my hand and tried to feed myself. Unfortunately, as I did, I smeared my face with mashed potato. Elsie simply wiped it off with a tissue and glanced at me before saying, 'Don't worry. It's all right, Paul. You'll get there eventually. Now try again.' I did, but this time the potato ended up all over my trousers. 'Not a good start,' I thought to myself.

After the day I'd had I was close to tears. I was missing my mother and I'd simply had enough. Elsie noticed, smiled, and then took the fork from me and said, 'Don't worry, Paul. We'll try again tomorrow.'

Looking back and thinking about it now, one thing sticks out for me from my first day. Unbelievably, I hardly did any lessons with going here, there and everywhere. I barely got to meet my teacher before I was off on my travels again. On reflection, I think rather than squash everything into one day, it would have been better to spread the therapy sessions over a couple of days as it was simply far too much for an eight-year-old boy to cope with.

At that particular time, I honestly couldn't remember being any sadder in my life than I was that night as I was put into bed by the night nurse. All I wanted was to go home to see my mother. Despite having these thoughts, I soon went to sleep. This was probably because of all the physical and mental strain I'd had on what was a truly eventful first day.

Chapter 9

AWAY FROM school, my father was sometimes very difficult; in fact more often than not he was. Despite this, I did spend time with him on the odd occasion.

Sometimes he would take me with him to places such as Ripon, Thirsk and Harrogate, all in North Yorkshire, to release his beloved racing pigeons for what's known in the trade as a 'toss' – in other words a trial flight. Looking back, I don't know why I agreed to go with him as I used to sit in the car for what seemed like hours, while he got his pigeons cleaned out and then ready to go. I think he only took me to have company on the trips, though who knows, I could be wrong. I have to say that once we actually got on the road, it was all right, but I absolutely hated the waiting beforehand. In the end, I stopped going with him for that reason.

I should explain that as briefly mentioned earlier in this book, my father was a pigeon fancier, and was right up until his death. At first he kept them in a loft at the back of our house. Before he married my mother, he also had them at home. In fact his mother once told me when one day when we were chatting that he'd kept pigeons in a shed in their backyard since he was 11 or 12 years old). But after complaints from the neighbours in Dundee Street after he married my mother, he moved them to an allotment with a newly built loft in it on Hundens Lane, which was about a mile from where we lived at the time. Thinking about it while I'm typing this, I honestly don't understand why he bothered, because more often than not his beloved pigeons failed to return to his loft after he released them. In some ways I felt sorry for him, because he did try hard, but something simply wasn't right. In all probability, his birds weren't good enough, a bit like Darlington in the 1972/73 season; they lost every week!

This was despite him spending considerable sums of money on his hobby. No matter how hard he tried, or how much money he wasted (interestingly my mother once pointed out that she had two or sometimes three jobs to keep the house going because he kept her short, yet he could always find money to fund his expensive hobby. I think this annoyed her immensely and rightly so in my opinion) the coveted rosette for first place usually eluded him. In the mid-1970s in order to try and improve his pigeon-racing fortunes, I remember that he came up with the idea of paying a well-known pigeon breeder called Massarella, who was based in Italy, several hundred pounds – which was a lot of money in those days – for a pair of birds which he intended to breed from. I think they must have been duds because his fortunes didn't improve in the slightest. I have to admit, I did find the whole episode both amusing and indeed annoying. Firstly it was funny (in a way) that his plan to breed 'super pigeons' – his words, not mine – went so badly wrong and secondly annoying because as I've mentioned my mother was working her fingers to the bone by having numerous jobs while he kept her short of money while indulging in this childish pipe dream of wanting the best pigeons. Now that I'm much older, I find what he did to be very selfish and in my opinion, it proved that his pigeons came ahead of his family.

Another interesting fact regarding his pigeons was that he used to keep his pigeon baskets in a cupboard under the stairs in our house. This is also where he stored his numerous bags of pigeon corn, which he used to buy in bulk in order to save money. This meant the place used to have a horrible musty smell and quite amusingly, when he opened the door, all the bags would topple forwards and spill their contents on the living room floor. I used to smirk to myself while he got on his hands and knees to pick it up off the grubby floorboards (the under the stairs bit) and spoon it back into the bags with his hands, rather than let it go to waste. Thinking about it, that's probably why his pigeons never won. They were probably full of dust and rubbish off the floor, as well as the dirty corn!

One final comment regarding the under-stairs cupboard: the aroma that escaped from the place when the door was opened probably wasn't helped by the fact that my father's old coat from when he worked at Shildon Shops in the 1960s was hanging up in there as well! Believe me, that coat stank. God knows why he kept it, as he never wore it during the whole of the 1970s. He no doubt thought that it would come in handy one day! I actually threw it out after he had passed away.

Returning to my father's pigeons, my grandfather (Frederick Hodgson, 1905–1978) came up with another reason why they didn't return to the loft. He claimed that this was because my father used to starve them by giving them the bare minimum amount of corn. I have to say in my father's defence that this can't have been true given the amount of pigeon corn (and dust from the floor) stashed under the stairs, even though it might have been a bit past its sell-by date by the time he came to feed it to them! Anyway, my grandfather perpetuated the myth of my father's stinginess by saying that the reason why they didn't return home was because they'd stopped off in a cornfield for a bite to eat! Maybe he was a bit tight with his pigeon corn, I'll never know for sure. I do know for a fact that he didn't starve them, though.

Before I tell you any more about my dad's pigeons, I need to say a few words about my grandfather. The phrase 'like father like son' might have described the two of them in certain respects, but one thing in particular was unique only to Frederick, and that was his compulsion for taking things to pieces – it wouldn't be too strong a word to say that he had a mania for it. As a child, I found his doing this at every opportunity highly amusing and when I think back, I still do to this day.

On one occasion, I recall that I was sitting in the front seat of my father's Ford Escort waiting for him to clean out his pigeons and sort some of them out to take for a 'toss'. As I've mentioned previously, this always seemed to take him an age. My grandparents lived just opposite Norman's allotment, so it came as no surprise to me when Frederick came out of his back door and into the driver's seat of my father's car and instantly proceeded to fiddle with the speedometer. In what seemed like no time at all, he had taken the whole thing apart. As I sat there next to him, I was amazed how quickly he had managed to achieve this task. However, actually putting it back together again was not one of his strongest points. When he eventually managed this, the glass on the clock was all crooked. He simply said, 'Don't worry, your dad won't notice.' He then added, 'See you later,' and got out of the car and back into his house. Of course my father did notice and said that I should have stopped him! 'What could I have done?' was my response. He didn't say another word and simply pulled a face.

On another occasion, I can remember when my grandfather actually managed to dismantle the driver's side door handle. Once again, it took him literally seconds to complete this task. Unfortunately, while putting it back together, he broke the handle and simply left all the pieces on the driver's seat before getting out of the car and leaving me to face the music. My father, quite rightly, blew his top when he discovered all the pieces of the handle on his seat. But rather than confront his father, once again, he blamed *me* for letting him do it! I honestly don't know how I could have stopped him though. I did say that if he hadn't taken almost two hours, he would have been back quicker and it wouldn't have happened. I also pointed out that I'd been waiting an hour prior to Frederick coming and doing his demolition job on the door handle. Once again, my father ignored my reasoning and pulled a face.

Cars, I suppose, in all shapes and sizes, were an obsession of my grandfather's. I recall that he owned a green Ford Anglia (as a kid I loved those cars, and even now would love one as even today, it is my favourite ever make of car. Incidentally, I have a couple of models in my bedroom which my wife Jen bought me) which I often saw parked in his driveway. The vehicle was regularly dismantled by my bungling grandfather, but the only problem he had was that he could never figure out where all the parts belonged when attempting to put it back together again. In the end he would get my cousin, Stephen, who was and indeed still is a mechanic, to put it back together again in order to get it moving. I lost count of the number of times that poor Stephen had to undertake this task. He must have dreaded the phone call asking for help!

When Frederick came to our house my model cars used to get the same rough treatment at his hands! I lost count of the number that had to be put in the bin following his visits. I did, however, get wise and when I knew that he was coming I took the precaution of hiding all my best ones!

Anyway, changing the subject, from what I can recall (remember it is almost 50 years ago, plus I was only a child at the time), I think my grandfather and grandmother had a bit of a love-hate relationship. Once, my grandmother told me about a ridiculous argument they had over the use of toilet paper. She made him use sheets of old newspaper while she kept the soft toilet roll for herself, guarding it jealously as if it was the Crown Jewels. This was because she claimed that he had once rolled a length of the precious toilet roll (in her mind precious) on the living room floor and then proceeded to flick his fag ash on it! Gleefully, she informed me that she didn't allow him to use toilet roll from that day and didn't do so until the day he died.

One final story regarding my father's pigeons that I feel I must tell you. It all started when a member of the public had found one of his birds and after reading the details on the identification ring on its leg, he then rang Hopetown and Whessoe pigeon club, the club my father was a member of and raced with. The secretary of the club contacted my father who in turn telephoned the man who had found his pigeon and arranged a convenient time to pick it up.

The two of us went to a house in the Skerne Park area of Darlington. For the reader unacquainted with

Darlington, I should explain that this council estate at that particular time had a really bad reputation for crime and problem families. Burglaries, for example, were rife. I certainly wouldn't have been on that estate after dark, that's for sure. On the plus side, these days it is apparently a far better place to live, so I have been told. I have often wondered if that is because the council has moved all the 'bad apples' out and put them somewhere else. I'll never know for sure, but I wouldn't be surprised if that were the case.

Anyway, back to my tale, and when we arrived at the address I sat in the car while my father went to the door as he, quite rightly, was frightened in case anyone stole it while he was in the house that he'd had the misfortune to enter. On looking around, my first impressions of the area were hardly favourable: the front of the house looked like a council rubbish tip; there was a wrecked car, with its doors missing, propped up on bricks on the lawn, surrounded by assorted junk (old toys, refuse, etc.). The grass was at least a foot high and there was no garden gate. When my father returned to the car, he said the interior was every bit as bad as the exterior. Apparently, the internal doors and the staircase had been chopped up and burnt on the fire – probably along with the garden gate – so the occupants used a cat ladder to get upstairs. During my father's conversations with the householder, it turned out that the copper water tank had been disconnected and sold to a scrap metal dealer! Basically, in my opinion, this family didn't deserve to have a council house and should have been evicted long before they had almost destroyed the property. I'm sorry to say, they were 'scruffs'. That's all I have to say about them.

During other excursions, my father would take me into his confidence and tell me about his job at Whessoe Engineering, where he was employed as a labourer. Whether he was pulling my leg or not, I don't know, but he certainly never tried to give me the impression that he was a model employee and would brag that he would sit on the toilet for hours on end reading the newspaper. Judging by his character, I think this was probably true. No wonder he eventually lost his job and never worked again from his early 50s.

Looking back now, I have to say that this was a shocking state of affairs. My father clearly didn't have his priorities right. Even at such a young age, I was determined not to follow his example and work as hard as I could in any future job I ended up doing. I honestly think that I managed to stick to that pledge I made to myself as a child, which is extremely satisfying.

Chapter 10

AFTER I'D been at Percy Hedley for almost a year, I still wasn't happy at all and as a result, I wasn't trying in my lessons or indeed my therapy sessions and overall I was a very unhappy little boy.

Looking back, I have to admit, all I wanted was to be at home and therefore back at Salters Lane School; so with this in mind, I wasn't interested in anything else, simply because my mind was set on that and that alone.

One particular incident happened, which was the straw that finally broke the donkey's back. Though reflecting on it now, it was probably a culmination of all the changes and indeed the constant unhappiness I'd endured during my first year at Percy Hedley School. Let me explain.

One morning, a frustrated Miss Carlisle was trying to fit me with some callipers (they went from the top of my legs to the bottom) as I wriggled like crazy in a vain attempt to stop her from putting them on me. No matter how hard she tried, the unfortunate physiotherapist couldn't get them on to my legs.

Calmly, Miss Carlisle said, 'Paul, keep still! I can't do this while you're constantly moving.' I frantically shook my head before stating, 'But they hurt, Miss. Stop it.' I then winced with pain and started to cry.

Miss Carlisle paused for a few seconds prior to explaining to me her reasons for fitting the callipers, 'Paul, these will help your legs get stronger. You want that, don't you? You won't have to wear them all the time. Just a couple of hours each day will be enough.' I continued to shake my head furiously before shouting, 'I don't want to wear them! I don't like it here. I want to go home! I hate you and I hate this school.' Miss Carlisle paused again and quickly realised that I was getting too upset to persist and therefore removed the callipers. She then said, 'All right, we'll leave it there for today, Paul. However, I have to say to you now, eventually you will have to wear them, whether you like it or not.' Without saying another word, she took me back to my classroom.

Later that night, I was laid in bed crying when a boy with learning difficulties called Malcolm (not his real name) came over to me and said, 'Don't cry, Paul. You will get used to it here soon.' I glared at him before angrily saying, 'No I won't! I've been here almost a year and I still hate it here! We are going to run away and you are going to help me.' Malcolm simply stood there, not knowing what to say or do, before eventually getting back into his own bed.

The following evening after tea, Malcolm was sitting on his bed, packing a carrier bag with some sweets, crisps and a bottle of pop as I looked on. He put the bag on the back of my wheelchair and then glanced at me before asking, 'Won't we get wrong, Paul?' I smirked then responded by stating, 'We'll only get into trouble if we get caught, my friend; which, hopefully, we won't. So come on, let's get going.'

Shortly after, Malcolm was pushing me along the corridor. In the distance, we heard footsteps heading in our direction. I paused for a couple of seconds and then pointed towards a storeroom door which was to our right (I think) and suggested, 'Quick! Let's hide in there. Whoever it is won't see us then.' The pair of us then quickly got into the storeroom without being seen, just!

From inside the storeroom, we heard the footsteps getting closer, then slowly, after a few seconds, they faded away, until eventually, they were gone. Once we knew for sure that the danger had passed, Malcolm opened the door and pushed me back into the corridor. I turned towards my friend and exclaimed, 'That was lucky. Come on, let's go, before anyone else comes.'

A few minutes later, Malcolm pushed me along the path and out through the main gates of the school.

Suddenly, a hand appeared on Malcolm's shoulder. He turned around and was shocked to see the headmaster behind him. He glared at us both before enquiring, 'And where do you think you're going to, my lads?' He then paused and said, 'Come on boys, let's get you both back inside.' Nothing else was said. We weren't shouted at, which looking back, surprised me.

So, that was the end of our adventure, or so I thought. How wrong I was!

The following Friday, my mother came to take me home for the weekend (my father must have been working or more likely seeing to his beloved pigeons because she had come on the train to pick me up). As we were about to leave, we were summoned to the headmaster's office by his secretary.

I can remember being glum-faced as I sat next to my mother, with the headmaster facing us both. He calmly explained what had happened, again without raising his voice. After he had finished talking, my mother, who incidentally, was horrified, glanced at me before asking, 'What made you do it, Paul?' I put my head down before responding by saying, 'I hate it here, mam. I want to go back to my other school and come home.' My mother gave me a stern look before saying in no uncertain terms, 'That can't happen, Paul. You are here to allow the staff to make you do as much as you can for yourself. So, hate it or not, you're staying here and if you don't start behaving yourself, you won't be going to any more football matches either. Do I make myself clear?' I reluctantly nodded before she continued, 'It's for your own good and just so you know, I never want to go through this again. I'm really disappointed with you.' I was utterly shocked by her words. They were like a knife to my heart and I never forgot them.

After a brief pause, the headmaster looked at my mother before stating, 'Well, thanks for coming in to see me today and for being so straight with Paul, Mrs Hodgson. I always think it is better coming from the parent.' He then paused for what seemed like the umpteenth time before continuing, 'I realise you have a train to catch so we'll leave it at that.' He then turned towards me, smiled and added, 'Right, Paul, enjoy your weekend, and we'll put all this behind us and start afresh on Monday. Is that all right with you?' My mother glared at me and then prompted me even further by prodding me in the arm. I jumped and then replied, 'Yes, Sir.'

The conversation I had that day really made me think and certainly partly changed my attitude towards school. I was also kept back a year through doing poorly in my lessons. So, in reality, both incidents convinced me to change my ways and indeed put more effort into everything.

Chapter 11

A FEW months after my telling off from my mother and the headmaster, our neighbour Mr Jones (not his real name) very kindly took me to a Darlington home match.

Once we got to Feethams, Mr Jones pushed me up past the cricket pitch towards the East Stand Paddock. I was proudly wearing my Darlington scarf that my mother had lovingly knitted me almost 18 months earlier.

After we had reached the paddock, we were sitting near the barrier which separated the stand from the playing surface, when Colin Sinclair, who was in the middle of warming up, spotted us and instantly sprinted in our direction, waving once during his ten-second journey.

In what seemed like no time, Colin joined Mr Jones and I at the barrier. He smiled at me prior to asking, 'Hi Paul, how are you doing at school? You mentioned briefly last time we spoke that you go to boarding school in Newcastle. I hope you are sticking in.' I returned the smile and said, 'Yes, I'm doing really well. I didn't like it at first but I now do.' Colin nodded, then looked towards Mr Jones. 'I bet you were a proud dad, weren't you, when Paul told you that he was doing well?' I laughed at the comment. Mr Jones smiled then replied by revealing, 'I'm not Paul's dad, I'm his neighbour and I offered to bring him along today to save his mother a job.' Colin grinned before saying, 'Oh, I'm sorry. I didn't realise.' Mr Jones smiled then said, 'Don't worry. It's an easy mistake to make.' Colin looked at us both before revealing, 'Nice to see you again, Paul.' He then paused for a couple of seconds before continuing, 'Good to meet you Mr?' Mr Jones smiled and then replied, 'Jones.' Colin nodded and then turned towards me, before revealing, 'I'm sorry Paul, but I really have to get back to the dressing room now as there's only 15 minutes until kick-off. But if you come to the players' entrance after the match, I'll have something for you.' With that and without uttering another word, he sprinted towards the players' tunnel and within a few seconds, he was out of sight.

I can remember being excited when I heard the crowd roar in celebration as the final whistle went. I turned to Mr Jones and said, 'I knew we'd win. I just knew it.' Shortly after I'd got over my excitement, the pair of us left the East Stand Paddock.

Within what seemed like no time, we were waiting outside the players' entrance. I was super excited as I wondered what Colin had for me.

The first player to come out was young Phil Owers. He stopped and smiled when he saw me and said, 'Hello

Paul. Good win today, eh?' I returned his smile before responding by saying, 'Hi Phil. Yes, it was, we'll get away from the bottom four yet. We are playing a lot better now.' Phil nodded and then stated, 'Of course we will; I'm sure of it. Anyway Paul, I have to dash. My girlfriend is waiting for me. We are going to her mother's house for tea. So, see you soon.' With that, he ran towards the car park. Once there, he jumped into a car, and within a few seconds he was heading out of the ground and out of my vision.

Shortly after Phil had left, Colin Sinclair appeared in the doorway. He smiled, 'Hi Paul. Did you both enjoy the match? It was a great win, wasn't it?' I nodded before replying by saying, 'Yes, it was brilliant. I'm over the moon that we won and you scored, which was even better.' Colin glanced at me prior to responding by replying, 'It was great to score, but the result is more important, as we really needed the points.' I nodded in agreement and then said, 'I get what you are saying, the result was far more important.'

A few seconds later, Colin took a programme out of his jacket pocket and handed it to me. My face lit up as I noticed all the signatures on the back of it. I then looked at Colin and excitedly said, 'Wow, thanks Colin. I'll keep this for ever.' Colin smiled and revealed, 'One other thing, before the next home game the manager said you both can come into the dressing room and meet the lads. They are all looking forward to seeing you.' By this time, I couldn't contain my excitement and exclaimed, 'I can't wait. I wish it was today!' Mr Jones smirked, and then glanced at Colin before saying, 'I can't thank you enough. You've really made Paul's day.' He then shook Colin's hand. Colin turned towards me and commented, 'You'll need to look after that programme. I'll try and get you a signed photograph of the team for next time I see you to go with it.' I looked up from reading my programme and replied, 'I look after all my programmes. They are in a box under my bed. It would be great if you could get me the signed photo, but I'm over the moon with this programme.' Colin smiled at my comment prior to saying, 'Anyway, you two, I have to go now.' He then looked at me before continuing, 'I'll see you at the next home match, Paul.' Once again, my face lit up as I revealed for the second time, 'I can't wait.'

An hour later, Mr Jones pushed me (wearing a huge smile on my face) into my living room. My father, who was sat in an armchair reading the paper, didn't acknowledge either of us and simply carried on with what he was doing. My mother, on the other hand, entered from the kitchen and smiled at Mr Jones before saying, 'Ah, Mr Jones, I thought I heard you. Would you like a cup of tea?' My father looked up from his paper and frowned before continuing with his read. Luckily, Mr Jones didn't notice his bad manners. However, my mother did; I could tell that she wasn't impressed in the slightest. Mr Jones responded by stating, 'Thanks Alice, but no. The wife will have my dinner ready shortly. So, I'll have to be going.' Alice then looked at me, smiled again and then asked, 'Did they win, then?' At that moment, I excitedly showed her my programme and revealed, 'Yes, we did. It was a brilliant result. Look what Colin Sinclair gave me. He got all the other players to sign it as well.' My mother and Mr Jones both grinned, each knowing that I'd had a really good day. Mr Jones then glanced at us both and revealed, 'I really have to go now. So, I'll leave you to it. Glad you had a good day, Paul. Bye Norman.' Norman simply grunted, without even lifting his head from his newspaper.

Thinking about it later, I didn't recall him turning the page once during the whole conversation with my mother, Mr Jones and I. I think he was simply being ignorant. Alice wasn't happy with his behaviour and shook her head in disgust before saying to Mr Jones, 'OK Mr Jones, thanks for taking Paul today. He's enjoyed himself judging by the look on his face.' Mr Jones smiled before stating, 'No problem Alice, anytime.' He then glanced at me prior to saying, 'See you later, Paul. Look after that programme, won't you.' I smiled and then said, 'I will Mr Jones, I promise, and thanks for taking me today. I really enjoyed myself. I can't wait for the next match. Hopefully we'll win again and don't forget, I'm meeting the team before the kick-off.' Mr Jones waved his arms in dismissive fashion then responded by saying, 'Yes, that will really be something for you to remember. Anyway, I'll see you all later.' With that, he headed out of the living room door.

Around 30 seconds later, after the front door had closed, my father put his newspaper down, looked at my mother and said with a frown on his face, 'Don't you be offering him a cup of tea. We don't want to encourage him, do we?' Alice, who obviously couldn't believe what she had just heard, glared at Norman prior to stating, 'I honestly can't believe you've just said that. Mr Jones has had your son out for the best part of the day while you've been sat on your fat backside doing nothing. And while I'm on, was there any need to be so ignorant? Paul and I know exactly what you are like, but there's no need to let all and sundry know. Sometimes, Norman, you are an absolute disgrace and you make me damned ashamed to know you.' This outburst must have hit a nerve because he simply put his head down without saying a single word and continued to 'read' his newspaper, while not for the first time my mother shook her head in disbelief.

Chapter 12

AS I mentioned earlier, I found being away from home quite a strain at first.

As I've also already said, Elsie Ferguson was a good 'housemother' – strict but fair. In fact she was a lot better than most of the other care staff who were employed by the school in my early days, some of whom, looking back, weren't very good at all, and seemed to do as little work as possible. (I'll go into this in more detail later.) All the same, I have to admit, I hated those early years at Percy Hedley. It was the feeling of being on my own that I didn't like, even though in reality I was surrounded by fellow pupils and members of staff, some of whom were caring and some not. In hindsight, it was no surprise that I was lonely and didn't fit in when I first started at Percy Hedley, but things did slowly get better for me which in turn made me much happier.

The object of going to a special school is to make you as independent as possible, and for me my school days certainly were an enlightening time (things happened along the way which I shall go into later), since they gave me the opportunity to prepare for my future role in the adult world. As you can imagine, the teachers were quite tough and in a way they had to be. However, although the discipline at Percy Hedley was very strict, it was only with the object of making the pupils as self-reliant as possible – which was a good thing. I cannot remember the cane ever being used as a punishment.

Away from school, my home life also still left a lot to be desired, but at least I was around people who were my family. Sadly, however, as you will probably realise by now, my father couldn't come to terms with my disability, so his absence while I was away was no great loss. I think he came to regret that; I could be wrong, but it was a feeling I got much later in my life. However, that's another story, one for another day. Instead, it was my mother who I missed more than anybody in the world when I was at Percy Hedley. These feelings of homesickness were diminished, to a certain extent, by the letters and money that she used to send me on a regular basis. Those letters certainly kept me going, particularly in my early days. The money she sent me was a bonus; hearing from her at least twice a week meant much more to me.

At first Alice had been over-protective towards me, but she soon learned the error of her ways. In no time at all her attitude had changed and she tried her best to teach me the importance of being resilient and self-sufficient. I never forgot her words and far more importantly her actions; they must have left a lasting impression on me and have benefitted me to this day.

However, returning to my story (again), when I used to return at the weekend from boarding school things never seemed to be right at home, and my mother was unhappy with her lot for much of the time. My father was often miserable and bad-tempered which must have got to her. Thinking about it now, I don't know why they got married. All my father seemed to be interested in was his pigeons rather than his family. I honestly feel that this attitude made him miss out on a lots, although at the time he didn't seem bothered. However, being like that was his decision, no one else's, therefore it was his loss and no one else's. Much later in life, this attitude resulted in him being a lonely old man near the end of his life with next to no visitors popping in to see him. Once again, that's a story for another day.

With all of the above taken into account, I have to say that in my opinion, my parents certainly were an ill-matched pair. In the early years of their marriage they would go out together at the weekend to Hopetown and Whessoe Working Men's Club and my grandmother (my father's mother) would come round to babysit. I really liked her. She actually unwittingly got me interested in family history, though I didn't know it at the time, when she told me how her mother (Margaret Fisher, 1877–1907) died when she was very young and her father who had the very odd name of Onesiphorus

Parslow (1866–1927), got remarried and she absolutely hated her stepmother.

In the last 20 years, I've taken up family history with the help of my good friend Ian Carter. After a lot of hard work, I have managed to trace my father's family (on his mother's side – i.e. the Parslows) right back to the 1600s. I am really pleased by this achievement.

Anyway, I must apologise for getting sidetracked yet again. Eventually, probably out of boredom, my mother no longer accompanied my father on these nights out. After this happened he would go out on his own for a drink and to play darts with his mates. This disappointed me in some ways as this meant my grandmother didn't come to visit as often and therefore we didn't have as many conversations about her younger days, which looking back now, was a real shame.

Although my home life could have been happier I never wanted for anything in material terms, given the fact that my father had a reasonably well-paid labouring job. That said, as mentioned earlier, he kept most of the money for himself, and my mother worked part-time in the town's indoor market on a leather goods store selling handbags and the like. When the need arose, she took on other jobs as well. Whatever the underlying cause of my parents' unhappiness might have been, it was definitely not due to a lack of money, apart from when my father was on the sick (this was mainly because my mother worked hard); though I should point out that Norman's reluctance to spend on the family did give rise to ill-feeling and resentment which, in fairness, despite the fact that I was really young at the time, I fully understood where this was coming from.

Chapter 13

THINGS CONTINUED to improve at school and my next positive turning point was when I was ten years old. Looking back, this was a huge achievement, though I have to admit that I didn't realise it at the time.

I can remember that I was wearing boots and callipers (yes, I did agree to wear them in the end, after a lengthy discussion with my mother about it) on this particular day. I lined myself up using the parallel bars and pulled myself out of my wheelchair into a standing position as Miss Carlisle watched closely.

With great determination, I managed to walk a few faltering steps.

All I could think about while I was doing this was the times that my father had put me down saying that I would never achieve anything in my life. Looking back now, I suppose in some ways, maybe he did me a huge favour because he certainly spurred me on to prove him wrong and improve my lot. All that went round in my head that particular day was his comment, 'You'll never amount to anything,' or words to that effect.

Anyway, Miss Carlisle smiled before saying, 'You see! You can do it. I always knew you'd be able to. I just knew it. Very well done, Paul; you've come a long way since you first came to see me and had to be propped up with cushions. I'm extremely proud of you and you should be extremely proud of yourself, as your hard work and indeed determination has got you this far.' I smiled excitedly at my achievement before exclaiming, 'Thanks Miss. That means a lot to me.'

A few days later, I was in feeding practice with Elsie. I can remember the day as if it were yesterday. I lifted a forkful of mashed potato into my mouth as Elsie watched. Not a bit was dropped down my clothes, nor was there any around my mouth. Elsie looked at me with a smile beaming right across her face. She then said, 'That's a lot better, Paul; very well done. I knew you would feed yourself properly one day. Everything takes time and your perseverance has certainly paid off.'

Pleased by my success, I pushed the cabbage to one side of the plate and attacked the mashed potato again. Elsie shook her head and stated, 'Now don't forget to eat your greens as well, will you.' After a brief pause, I reluctantly prodded the cabbage with my fork, pulling a face before putting it into my mouth. Elsie smiled once more before saying, 'Good lad.' Her smile confirmed to me that what she'd just said was indeed correct and all our hard work had paid off. No more wearing my food either around my face, or all down my trousers. I can remember being very happy that day. I was more pleased with this achievement than the parallel bars one, probably because I knew I'd never walk properly and being able to feed myself without making a mess seemed a lot more useful to me. Incidentally, my feelings haven't changed. I still feel the same way today. I absolutely hate dropping food either on the table, or on the floor.

Now it's time for me to go into more detail on how Miss Birrell helped me with my speech.

It all started when she found out that I was a Darlington supporter. Very cleverly, she put this to good use.

One day, we were in her speech therapy room when she held a card on which was written in capital letters 'THE QUAKERS ARE MY FOOTBALL TEAM'. She then said, 'Now, Paul – deep breath.' I inhaled a lungful of air before making my first attempt, 'The – Qua – kers – are …' Miss Birrell then said, 'Now, take another deep breath, Paul.' Again, I inhaled deeply and the following words emerged from my mouth, 'My – foot – ball – team.' Miss Birrell patted me on my shoulder before exclaiming, 'Brilliant, Paul. Well done. I can't believe how much your speech has improved and it's all down to your hard work and perseverance.' I smiled, then responded by saying, 'And your patience; especially in those early days when I was struggling with being here. I'll never forget what you have done for me.'

I'm still in touch with Miss Birrell to this day and only recently I reminded her how grateful I was for the assistance she gave me with my speech. I think she was taken aback to be honest.

Anyway, In order to consolidate and indeed improve my speech, I started reading football magazines such as *Shoot!* and *Match* out loud almost every night. Doing this regularly helped me greatly and brought my speech on no end and it was something that I really enjoyed doing. However, I know for certain that without Miss Birrell's help, I wouldn't be where I am today; that's why I'm so eager to sing her praises to anyone who will listen!

After so much improvement in my condition my mother continued to support me, but in his stubborn way my father still couldn't bring himself to show me any attention or praise my achievements. And thinking back as I'm typing this, it hurt me at the time so much for him not to take pride in his son getting visibly better by the week. Every time I went home after my initial struggles, I could do something that I couldn't before. Not surprisingly, my mother spotted this straight away and was genuinely pleased. Unfortunately, my father simply wasn't interested.

As I mentioned earlier, I think he regretted it later, but at that time, it would have meant the world to me to hear him say, 'Well done.' Unfortunately, I never did hear those two words.

Chapter 14

WHEN I was nine years old, I became friendly with a teacher called Mr O'Dowd. All the teachers had to do one late shift per week. It was during one of these that Mr O'Dowd mentioned to me about playing chess. Over the next few months, he taught me how to play the game and over the years I actually turned out to be a very good player. Unfortunately, since I left school in 1981, I've hardly played, which looking back is a real shame. However, I have fond memories of those chess games and the time that Mr O'Dowd gave me.

I can remember my mother bought me a chess set when I first started to play, but for some strange reason someone stole both of my Queens. I was really upset about this at the time because my prized chess set was ruined. Whoever stole the pieces probably simply threw them away, as they would be no good to them whatsoever. This made it more annoying. My mother complained to Elsie, but nothing was ever done and the culprit was never caught.

Regarding Mr O'Dowd, I shall go into a lot more detail about him later in this book.

At around this time, something not as nice happened to me. Let me try to explain.

There was an older lad in school who shall remain nameless because of the reasons given below. He was a nasty piece of work and looking back, he was a sexual predator. He was around 13 at the time and was a big lad.

Anyway, I had the misfortune to come into contact with him one day when I was using a urine bottle. He came into the toilet, took the bottle away and started to touch me. I was totally taken aback and froze. I was actually quite frightened. Luckily for me, we heard footsteps coming in our direction and he ran off, leaving me somewhat confused. Being nine years old I thought his behaviour was very strange to say the least, but I didn't tell anyone.

A couple of weeks later (I think it was a couple of weeks), I was reading a book in the dormitory when he came in. He said, 'I want to see you naked on your bed.' I told him to get lost but again, he tried to touch me. Keeping calm, I said, 'I'm sure that you know who my best friend is?' The boy shook his head and replied, 'No.' I smiled and simply revealed, 'Malcolm.' Suddenly, he paused for a few seconds and then left the dormitory without saying another word. I knew this boy was scared of Malcolm, so my quick thinking probably saved me from a possible sexual assault. Not that I knew it at the time; however, I did know that something certainly wasn't right.

The next day, I told Malcolm what had happened (I'm not sure whether he understood) and said that we needed to teach this lad a lesson. Malcolm agreed to threaten him, which he did. Luckily I was never bothered by this predator again.

I have to admit that I had been scared but through a bit of luck (the footsteps coming towards the toilet) and standing up to this piece of filth, I wasn't harmed. It was only later, when I knew more about sex, that I realised how bad it could have been for me if I hadn't nipped it in the bud, with the help of my friend.

There were other rumours about this individual and shortly after he was moved to a different school. Good riddance as far as I was concerned.

Some years later, I was contacted by the police regarding this scumbag. Apparently, other incidents had been brought to their attention. I told them exactly what had happened to me but he was never found. Therefore nothing came of it, which was a great shame. The guy knew exactly what he was doing and deserved to be punished. Unfortunately, to this day, he never has been.

Chapter 15

WHEN I was 11, I moved into the secondary section of the school.

This is where I came into contact with a teacher who shall remain nameless for the first time. I have to say that it came as a huge shock to me, especially after the kindness Mr O'Dowd and my form teacher Mrs Moore had shown me. I'll go much deeper into that later though.

By this time, my speech had become a lot clearer. As I alluded to earlier, when I started Percy Hedley School in 1973, hardly anyone could understand what I was trying to say. I did have an acute speech impediment and I was amazed at the marked improvement, which was down to my own hard work and the patience of my speech therapist, Miss Birrell.

At this time I also excelled at my schoolwork, especially English, which I loved.

In addition, at around 12 years of age I had reached my physical peak, so to speak, and was told that I wouldn't improve physically any further. I no longer had to wear callipers by this time, which was much more comfortable. In addition, this also meant that I could wear normal shoes, rather than the horrible boots that the callipers were attached to. I can remember my mother taking me to buy my first pair of shoes in five years. I was really excited and chose a brown pair with a little wedge on. I loved those shoes!

As well as my physical improvements, by the time I was 12 I could wash and dress myself, clean my teeth and feed myself, things which my doctor, as well as my father, said I would never be able to do. I also only needed speech therapy about once a month, which again, thinking about it now, was a great achievement.

Speaking of being 12, I remembered that birthday for a special reason. Let me explain more.

I can remember Elsie watching as I opened a birthday card emblazoned with a gold number 12, which contained a £5 note. I gazed at the banknote before looking at my housemother and saying, 'Look, Miss! I've got five pounds from my mam.' Elsie smiled and then responded by stating, 'So, what are you going to spend it on, Paul?' I pondered for a few seconds, and then replied, 'A radio, Miss! Then I can listen to the Darlo matches after lessons.' Elsie smiled again before saying, 'That sounds like a plan.' She then smirked before stating, 'You and that football club. You are Darlo-mad.' That comment certainly made me smile, as by this stage in my life I'd become a Darlington fanatic.

At around this time I represented the school at various disabled sporting events such as the wheelchair dash, wheelchair slalom and, more dangerously, throwing the javelin. Letting me hold such a sharp implement was surely a recipe for disaster – once I accidentally dropped it and nearly impaled my foot! Rob, who was far more disabled than me, actually did. I didn't really enjoy these games. They simply weren't my thing. Despite this, I tried my best and did fairly well and to this day I still have the certificates I won. Many of these were firsts. One final comment on these events: they were called 'The Spastics Games'. How times change! Language like that wouldn't be tolerated now, that's for sure.

Also, I was introduced to pottery, art and cookery. I hated pottery and art and even today still think that for a person with my disability, they were a complete waste of time in my humble opinion. Two questions that I often asked myself at the time were, 'Was I ever going to make plates, or ornaments using pottery for a living?' Answer, 'No.' 'Did I have aspirations to be an artist?' Answer, 'No.' Personally, I would have much preferred to have got on with English and maths in the classroom. Instead, I ended up being clarted up to the eyeballs with either clay or paint. I tried my best to do these subjects, but my heart simply wasn't in them. More importantly, I physically couldn't do them. Looking back, doing pottery and art resulted in many hours being wasted, hours that could have been spent doing something more useful. Thinking about it, time is precious; with this in mind, you should never waste it as you'll never get it back again once it has gone. I've always tried to remember that throughout my life.

I fully understood the reasons behind me doing cookery. However, even this in my opinion wasn't done correctly by the staff at the school. For example, why get severely disabled kids to try and make a Christmas cake? On one occasion, my mother bought the ingredients for me to make one. They weren't cheap either. Anyway, the teacher showed us how to make the cake. She then rather foolishly expected the kids like Rob and I to make their own.

It goes without saying that us physically disabled kids struggled. Despite my best efforts, my bowl, together with its contents, ended up on the floor. Mine wasn't the only one! As a result, all the ingredients were wasted. Luckily for me, my mother bought me more than enough to make one cake so I did eventually create one of sorts! Later, after eating a piece, my mother said it was 'nice'. To this day, I don't know whether she was being polite or not!

Surely, a better way of doing this exercise would have been for Rob and I to watch the teacher make her cake or follow the recipe from a book then tell her what to do. Most of these kids would never be able to bake a cake themselves, but if they had the knowledge, in theory, they could show an able-bodied person (for example a personal assistant) how to do it. When I told my mother what happened to most of my ingredients, she wasn't impressed in the slightest, especially as my father wasn't working at the time (yet again) and she had scrimped and saved to buy them for me. She agreed with my point of view and said that it would have been better all round if the teacher had baked the cake under my instruction.

Staying with cookery, here are a couple of stories that occurred while I was doing the subject.

Firstly, a lad with learning difficulties dropped two eggs on the floor. The teacher told him to clean the mess up, but didn't explain to him how to do it. The lad proceeded to try and clean up with a dustpan and brush. As a result, there was egg from one end of the kitchen to the other. Just then another teacher came into the room and proceeded to slip once she stood in the egg and ended up skidding across the room before ending up on her backside! Looking back, I have to say that it was really funny. Actually, I still smile when I think about it to this day. It was like a sketch from *Benny Hill.* Luckily for her, the teacher who slipped was all right; though thinking about it, she could have injured her back or anything. After she had gone, the cookery teacher glared at the young lad and yelled, 'You stupid boy!'

The lad was obviously very upset. However, if you think about it logically, it wasn't really his fault because if the teacher had thought about it and told him to clean the mess up with a cloth (or better still, showed him) rather than leave him to his own devices, the incident would certainly have been avoided. In addition, even in the mid-1970s, calling someone with learning difficulties 'stupid' wasn't right and certainly wouldn't be tolerated in today's society and rightly so in my opinion. Even in those days when attitudes were far different than they are today, the teacher could and probably should have chosen her words better. Taking it a step back further though, if she'd done her job properly, the incident wouldn't have happened and then she wouldn't have lost her temper in the first place.

The second occurrence was when another lad (again with learning difficulties) was boiling milk to make some custard. After a few minutes, the milk started to boil over. However, once this had started to happen, rather than turn the hob off, to my amazement he proceeded to watch the whole contents of the pan end up all over the cooker! Again, the teacher told him off and called him 'useless'. But as in the first case, she didn't give him the correct instructions, to turn the cooker off once the milk was bubbling. If she'd done that, she wouldn't have ended up with a messy cooker to clean, as well as a pan with a hole in it that had to be thrown out with the rubbish. Really these two incidents showed the complete lack of training the teacher must have had regarding children with learning difficulties. If she had been properly trained, she would have had the knowledge and indeed knowhow to handle both of these incidents much better.

The final story concerns my own efforts on the cookery front. I had made some cheese scones but instead of adding a pinch of salt to the mix I had put in a good handful. I then took them home and told my mum not to eat any.

My dad loved cheese scones and much to my amusement, he grabbed one and took a big mouthful. Within a matter of seconds, he then proceeded to spit it out while I was shaking with laughter. To his credit, for once in his life, he did see the funny side of this practical joke and even laughed. Later, when he'd gone to the club, my mother remarked how well he had taken it. I have to admit, I was shocked and indeed surprised as well.

Away from cookery, in my first year of secondary school one of my favourite subjects was social studies. What I particularly liked was that in that first year we used to visit old people in their homes in Forest Hall.

I befriended a man called Mr Arrol and as far as I can remember, I was the only person he would allow in to see him out of the whole of my year. He liked me and I liked him. He used to tell me about his exploits during the Second World War. He was on the Normandy beaches on D-Day. I found this really interesting as my grandfather George Wood was also involved on 6 June 1944, despite being almost 40 years old (my mother told me during one of our many conversations that he was one of the oldest privates there).

Anyway, back to Mr Arrol. I loved going to see him and always looked forward to going to it. As well as talking about the war, we also used to play Scrabble together. He was very good at it and beat me nine times out of ten.

When I moved up to the second year, I couldn't go and see him any more. I was really disappointed by this but I did write to him until he passed away several years later.

I have to say that my friendship with Mr Arrol and the pleasure we both derived from each other's company provided a stark contrast to that of my own father. Despite being used to his attitude towards me by this time, it still made me think what could have been.

One final thought for this chapter. It was at around this time that I became more aware of girls. Much later, a thought occurred to me. People think we exaggerate when we equate places such as Percy Hedley School with Victorian principles, but adult institutions frowned on intimate relationships between disabled couples. If this was frowned on between adults, it was also a big no-no between adolescents. Girls were housed at the top of the school and boys at the bottom and they never were allowed to meet. After all, the above lessons had to be learned early (maybe later in life, they didn't want disabled people to breed, so if this was indeed the case, the rule, in theory, could have been the start of that). It goes without saying that we always found ways around this unwritten law and managed to mingle.

I have to say that this outdated thinking wouldn't be tolerated today and looking back, it shouldn't have been then either!

Chapter 16

NOW IS the time to tell you about the teacher who spoiled much of my time in secondary school.

But first as you may recall, Mr O'Dowd was really kind to me and helped me greatly with my maths and as I mentioned earlier, he also taught me to play chess and I spent many happy hours pitting my wits against him. Eventually I improved sufficiently to beat him on a regular basis, which really pleased me as I'd gone from someone who couldn't play the game at all and didn't even know the names of the pieces, to where I eventually found myself after only a few months. After I'd beaten him for the first time, he said that I'd picked the game up really well, which was good to hear.

On a separate note, I was also extremely grateful to him for the one-to-one tuition that he gave me which resulted in me passing my CSE in arithmetic. I have to admit that I had to put a lot more work into this because while English seemed to come to me naturally, arithmetic certainly didn't. Looking back, I think that's the reason I took more satisfaction from passing my arithmetic, rather than my three English examinations.

Many years after I'd left school, I met Mr O'Dowd at a reunion. When he learned that I'd got a job in the civil service, he said the reason that he spent so much time with me was that he saw that I was bright and had potential. He added that too many disabled young adults were content to leave school and spend the rest of their time in residential care rather than getting off their backsides and doing something with their lives. His words, not mine. That's a discussion for another day (I do however agree with this sentiment, as I've seen this for myself), but I certainly took what he said about me as a compliment and it meant a lot to me as it came from a man I really respected.

Unfortunately, Mr O'Dowd is no longer with us. When I heard of his passing, it saddened me greatly because I really liked him, simply because he gave me a lot of his time (on many occasions much more than he had to) over the years, something that I'll always be grateful to him for.

Mrs Moore, my English teacher, was also very kind to me. She quickly noticed that I was good at the subject and encouraged me from day one. Once again, I was really grateful for the extra time that she afforded me. When it came to taking my CSEs, just like Mr O'Dowd with my arithmetic, she played a huge part in me achieving my English language, English literature (the book I studied was *The Midwich Cuckoos* by John Wyndham who is far better known for writing *The Day of the Triffids*) and English oral.

Thinking about it now, Mrs Moore's help probably set me up on my later writing career as it was through her diligence that I discovered my latent skill and love for writing. Although I didn't know it at the time!

Mrs Moore also passed away several years ago and once again, I was sad when I heard the news.

I'd like to say some more about this brilliant teacher. She introduced us to theatre, taking us to see Gosforth Amateur Dramatic Society perform *The Winslow Boy* and indeed many other plays.

Even now, I look back on those days with great fondness.

Every Christmas she would commit to directing the senior classes' Christmas play which was performed in front of admiring parents. Can you imagine trying to school a horde of petulant, uninspired, rebellious disabled teenagers into performing Charles Dickens's *Oliver Twist* and other classics? But by hook or by crook, every year, she managed to pull it off. I have to say that, thinking about it now, I really admire her for achieving this feat year after year.

Another thing for which I shall be for ever indebted to Mrs Moore was my first introduction to social justice. When we were in her class we would be paired up and sent to visit old people in their homes. As I mentioned earlier in this book, I was paired with Mr Arrol, whom I got on with extremely well.

I have to say that Mrs Moore and Mr O'Dowd were special to me in a good way, not in a 'different' way.

Unfortunately, in all walks of life no matter where you are, whether it be at work, college, football matches or school, there's always a bad apple and I met mine in the secondary school section at Percy Hedley.

I won't mention his name but this teacher definitely had his favourites. I quickly found out that I wasn't one of them. His reasoning for this was he bought a piano from the school which previously had been used for music lessons with Mrs Moore. Anyway, in one such lesson, a boy with learning difficulties decided to put some hardback books down the back of the piano. The end result was that when Mrs Moore started to play it, no sound came out. The whole class, including Mrs Moore, found this highly amusing. Once the laughter had subsided, the books were removed, the music lesson commenced and nothing else was said.

I have to admit, I did laugh and like the rest of the class, I did egg the boy on to put the books in the piano, as we all thought it would be funny. So, basically, I was part of the childish prank, along with the whole class.

Anyway, after this unnamed teacher had purchased the piano from the school, he found out about the prank from one of his favourites and from that day, he disliked me as a result.

To this day, I don't know why he singled me out of the whole class. It baffled me then and it still does now. Maybe he was looking for someone to blame, I don't know. Later, I found out that the books had damaged the piano and it couldn't be repaired; therefore this teacher had wasted his money. I have to admit, I did smile to myself when I heard this news.

Three incidents concerning this individual stick in my memory; there were many more but these three will suffice for this book.

In the mid-1970s, my mother unfortunately got cancer and was taken into hospital. So for one or two weekends I had to stay at school.

The first weekend, this teacher was on weekend duty. 'Just my luck,' I thought. The staff knew about my mother and that I was really worried about her. Anyway, I was in the TV room one afternoon on my own reading a book and minding my own business when this teacher appeared behind me and whispered, 'The real reason that you are here for the weekend is that your parents don't want you, so they dumped you on us.' He then smirked before leaving the room.

I was very upset by this and at dinner time, Elsie, who was also on weekend duty, noticed and asked if I was all right. I said that I was just worried about my mother. She said that I should try not to worry and if I wanted to talk to her I could. I thought that was really caring of her. I never did tell anyone what that teacher had said to me that day. But now as an adult, thinking back, what a despicable thing to say to a child already in turmoil over his mother's health. He didn't even have the excuse that he didn't know that my mother was seriously ill, because all the staff did. Even if by any chance he hadn't known, it was still an unforgivable thing to say to a child. The following weekend Mr O'Dowd was on weekend duty. He took me to the shops to buy a get well card for my mother. We then wrote it out together and posted it. What a difference seven days made. More importantly in my opinion, this really showed the difference between the two men!

One final comment on this incident: once my mother had recovered, I told her what the teacher had said. She was furious and wanted to complain to the headmaster. I informed her that there wasn't anyone else in the room so therefore he'd deny it and it would end up making my dealings with this guy even more difficult than they already were. My mother, probably against her better judgement, went along with what I wanted and no complaint was ever made.

My mother fully recovered and lived for almost another 20 years. No one was happier than me when I got the news by letter. I can remember for some reason my aunty had written to the headmaster with the news, rather than me. He came to my class, took me to his office and gave me the good news as well as the letter. I'll never forget that day. Funnily enough, on the way to his office, I kept on thinking, 'What have I done?' as the headmaster didn't say a word during the whole of the journey. The scene was surreal but I was a relieved young man as the headmaster took me back to my class.

Anyway, I'm digressing yet again, so I had better get back to my story. The second incident was two years later when our class had some worms which were being studied in our biology lesson. Malcolm cut them up for some reason. At the time it happened, I knew he was the culprit, but I didn't have a clue why he'd done it and if I'd known beforehand, I certainly would have stopped him.

I can honestly say that I had nothing to do with it. Later, Malcolm told me that he wanted to see if they still moved when they were cut up. I already knew that they did.

Anyway, despite having no reason to do so (apart from his obvious dislike of me), this teacher blamed me. He proceeded to take me up to the art room, which was on another floor of the building, where we were on our own and said, 'You cut the worms up, didn't you?' I replied that I wouldn't be able to do it as I wouldn't be able to hold the knife still enough. He paused for a few seconds and then said, 'All right. Fair enough, but you got one of the kids who aren't very bright to do it for you, didn't you? I know you are telling lies; just like you lied about being responsible for damaging my piano.' I said that I honestly knew nothing about it. To my horror the teacher put his face right up against mine and shouted, 'You are a lying little shit.' By this time I was scared out of my wits and said that I knew nothing about the worms and I reminded him of the fact that the whole class played the piano prank on Mrs Moore. By this time I was white and the teacher realised that he'd gone too far. He let go of my throat and said, 'If you ever tell anyone what happened today, you'll regret it.' He then took me back to the classroom without saying another word. Later, to his credit, Malcolm owned up. But I never did get an apology. Interestingly, the teacher didn't tell him off, as I found out when I asked Malcolm later. He was simply told, 'Don't do it again.'

That night Elsie, whose bedroom was near the art room, said that she'd heard a commotion and almost came to see what was happening. I said it was 'nothing'. I could tell that she didn't believe me but it was never mentioned again. As far as I know, I think she also asked the teacher concerned what had happened. He also said that it had been nothing.

A few days after the incident, I was playing chess with Mr O'Dowd. We were chatting while setting up the pieces, and I very nearly told him what had happened, but something stopped me and I never told anyone for years. Looking back now, I should have done but I thought that I wouldn't have been believed. I know one thing, if I'd told my mother, she'd have been on the next train to the school demanding answers as to why I was being bullied in this way. She certainly wouldn't have let it rest and would have gone to the education department if she wasn't happy with any explanations given. Unfortunately, because I kept quiet about what had happened to me, she never got that opportunity.

The final incident actually gave me some satisfaction after all the bullying and abuse I'd taken from this man. I was almost ready for leaving school and this teacher said, 'You'll end up in a day centre, mark my words, because people like you always do.' I responded by saying, 'That won't happen. Luckily I've had brilliant support from Mr O'Dowd and Mrs Moore. I've had none whatsoever from you. I don't know how you dare call yourself a teacher. You are a disgrace to the profession.' Or words to that effect. Before he could answer, I simply left the room, leaving him open-mouthed and stuck for words.

Looking back, to this day I still find it absolutely unbelievable that a grown man could have so much pent-up hate towards a child over a damaged piano. It must have been on his mind constantly. To be fair, if I'd acted on my own with regard to the piano incident, then maybe I could understand, but that wasn't the case.

At the time I found his behaviour pathetic. After suffering at this teacher's hands for almost five years, I honestly think that he had some kind of mental problem. He should never have been allowed to teach disabled, or indeed any other children, in my opinion.

Much later, after hearing from other former pupils, it quickly became apparent that this teacher had bullied and made dozens of other kids' lives a complete misery. Not one, including me, spoke out at the time and none of us knew that anyone else was suffering sustained bullying from this guy. We all thought that we were the only ones. This, in my opinion, makes this all the sadder. Maybe if I'd spoken up, others would have. However, I'll never know now.

At least after talking to them I knew that I wasn't the only one, which made me feel better.

Chapter 17

IF ANYONE thinks that my life in secondary school was miserable all the time, then they are wrong. As when I was away from that teacher I discussed in the last chapter of this book, I put his behaviour to the back of my mind and simply made the best of things.

Here are a couple of memorable incidents that spring to mind from around that time.

One day, representatives from a local shooting club visited our school. One of them handed me a pistol and told me to shoot at a target which was situated a few feet in front of me. (I think it was a few feet, though I can't remember the exact distance.) Unfortunately, at a most inopportune time, I had a spasm attack, which made my hand shake. The end result was that I almost took out one of the instructors when I fired just over his head. His face was an absolute picture. Thinking about it, it would have made a fantastic scene in a film! Sorry, that's my filmmaker mode coming to the fore. Anyway, returning to my tale, he quickly took the gun off me and had a swift rethink and said, 'I don't think that was a very good idea, Paul.' Obviously they weren't using live ammunition, but it would have still caused significant damage if someone had been hit at such a close range.

This incident just goes to show that some disabled people are far better off holding conversations than guns. Such people should be encouraged in the classroom to improve their lot, as I've already alluded to in this book. They shouldn't be forced to scramble in the mud where they are a danger to themselves and others, which I obviously was that particular day. Nevertheless, despite this fact, I still find the whole episode highly amusing and I still smile when I think about it today.

One final thought on this incident: like so many that happened while I attended Percy Hedley School, this one certainly would not have been allowed to happen today simply because of Health and Safety rules.

It was also around this time that I started playing the card game three card brag (for money) with some other kids of my age in my room. I must stress that we'd never let the younger kids play because it would have been unfair to take money from them.

On this particular occasion, I was having a really good night and my winnings were neatly heaped up in front of me.

Malcolm stood behind me, watching the game as he slurped from a can of lager and in between, ensuring that my piles of coins were stacked up neatly.

In this particular hand, there was only me and a lad called Benny (not his real name), who was a year younger than me and had slight learning difficulties, left. The other two players had thrown their hands in. I glanced at Benny and said, 'Let us see what happens if I raise you 50 pence, my friend.' Benny looked surprised and replied, 'What?' I responded by reiterating, 'You heard me; 50 pence.' I then took a drink from my can of lager and watched the expression on Benny's face. Unfortunately for me, I squeezed the can that little bit too hard and at that very moment, Benny noticed the tell-tale nervous spasm in my hand. Benny smirked before stating, 'I know you're bluffing! I'll see you.'

Dismayed and indeed angry with myself for giving the game away (in more ways than one), I revealed my cards which contained nothing higher than a ten of spades. For those who don't know the game, that is 'ten high' and therefore is a very poor hand. Benny unveiled his hand, which was a pair of queens. He gleefully scooped up his winnings. Due to me having a spasm at an inopportune time, my bluff had failed and I'd lost around £5; a lot of money in those days. I was gutted as I watched Benny pocket all his winnings. After that, I never took a drink from a can during a card game and I won a lot more than I lost.

As Benny was scooping up his money, a trainee carer called Julie entered the room and glanced at us before revealing, 'I'd put those cans and the money you have piled up there out of sight if I were you, lads. Elsie is doing her rounds.' I smiled and said, 'Thanks for letting us know, Julie.' Julie returned my smile before replying, 'No problem.' She then left the room, closing the door behind her.

I looked at my fellow card players and said, 'I thought someone was keeping watch? Malcolm, get rid of those cans, will you? I'm just off to the toilet.' I quickly grabbed my money and headed towards the bedroom door. After I'd left the room, unbeknown to me at the time, Malcolm had foolishly stowed the clinking carrier bag, full of cans, on top of my wardrobe. I only found this out later when he told me that he'd panicked and didn't think.

On my return from the toilet, I was both shocked and dismayed to find Elsie pouring a can of our lager down the other bathroom sink with Malcolm and Benny looking on, glum-faced.

Elsie glanced at me and smirked prior to stating, 'Ah, Paul; nice to see you. Come in and join the party. Do you know anything about this?' I shook my head and then replied, 'No Miss; I swear I don't. All this is news to me.' I stared hard at Malcolm who then looked sheepishly at Elsie and revealed, 'I bought them, Miss. Paul didn't know anything about it. I hid them in his room rather than mine.' Elsie replied, 'Did you, young man? You must think I was born yesterday. I don't believe you at all, but I've got no proof. Either way, I think I'm going to have a word with the man in the off-licence and tell him to stop selling you lager.' My housemother then turned her attention to me and said, 'And as for you Paul, I don't think you are as innocent in all this as you make out, in fact I know you're not, so, I'm going to put a stop to your antics once and for all. I'm putting Stephen Young [not his real name] in with you from next week.' I screwed up my face before saying, 'Oh God. No, not him.' Elsie smirked and then nodded her head. She then added, 'That will teach you a lesson, young man.'

One final comment regarding the cans of lager: I gave Malcolm £5 for taking the blame. He was over the moon!

I shall explain the impact of Elsie's decision in the next chapter.

Chapter 18

TWO WEEKS later, I had my first bad experience of sharing a room with Stephen.

Here is what happened on that fateful occasion. (Once again, I couldn't remember word for word; however, the facts are correct.)

I was woken up one night when I heard a really loud breaking of wind coming across from the other side of the room where Stephen was in bed. At first, I couldn't believe what I'd just heard. After a few seconds, I sat up and said to my roommate, 'Stephen, you bloody well stink to high heaven. Is there any need for that?' He looked across the room before revealing, 'I've shit the bed, Paul.' I shook my head in utter disbelief and asked, 'You have done what?' He confirmed what he'd just said by saying, 'Shit the bed.' I was fuming as the smell was making me feel sick and I responded angrily by stating, 'You dirty get. There's absolutely no need for that. You should've shouted the night staff.' Stephen smiled before pointing out, 'I did it on purpose. I even had to force one out.' I honestly couldn't believe what I was hearing and by this time I was even more annoyed than I was before. So I enquired, 'What the hell did you do that for? I can't get my head around why you'd mess yourself on purpose. It's a stupid, filthy thing to do.' Stephen smirked prior to revealing, 'To get the night nurse back for telling me off earlier.' I sat up in bed and said, 'You are an idiot, Stephen.' I then shouted very loudly, 'Miss!'

A couple of minutes later, I squinted my eyes as the light was switched on.

The night nurse entered the room and sniffed the air. She then asked, 'Has one of you had an accident?' I shook my head and replied, 'Not me, Miss.' She nodded and then smiled at me before heading towards Stephen's bed. She pulled back the covers and then shook her head in temper. She then looked him in the eye and stated, 'Stephen! All you needed to do was shout me and then all this could have been avoided.' A falsely embarrassed Stephen responded by saying, 'Sorry Miss.' The night nurse glared at him and shouted, 'Sorry doesn't wash any more, Stephen. Anyway, I'll be back in a minute.' She then left the room, muttering to herself on her way up the corridor. I looked at Stephen and asked, 'Where has she gone?' Stephen replied, 'To get the bucket and sponge to wash me down.' I was shocked and asked, 'You are joking?' Stephen shook his head and replied, 'No, unfortunately not.'

Sure enough, five minutes later the night nurse returned, carrying a bucket of water and a sponge, and she glared at Stephen before saying, 'Come on. Let's get those dirty pyjamas off.' She then pulled Stephen's pyjamas off and simply dropped them on to the floor. A few seconds later, she proceeded to lift him up, in order that she could pull the soiled sheet off his bed. Once she had done that, she again threw it on to the floor. Having had to witness this, it goes without saying that I had a frustrated look on my face, and I stated, 'Do you have to do that here? It absolutely stinks. And it's not exactly something that I want to see. Why don't you just put him in the bath? That to me would be the best solution all round.' The night nurse glanced at me, shook her head and replied, 'This way is much quicker. I have other children to look after as well as him.' I was somewhat surprised by this comment and asked, 'What about his dignity?' She quickly looked back at me before responding, 'He should've thought about that before he did this. I wasn't born yesterday; I know exactly what he's up to. I'll tell you another thing, if it was up to me he could lay in his own mess until the morning. However, I want to keep my job. That's the only reason I'm doing this now.' I nodded. Then she continued by stating, 'I honestly don't mind when some kids have accidents as some of them genuinely can't help it. I clean them up as it is part of my job. But when someone messes themselves on purpose, it really annoys me as it gives me extra work that I don't need. I have over 30 kids to look after. It has a knock-on effect, as I'll be late doing my checks to make sure everyone is all right. Unfortunately Stephen doesn't think of that when he gives me all this unnecessary work.' I nodded and then replied, 'I fully understand where you are coming from. It must be very frustrating for you.' She ended the conversation by revealing, 'That's a huge understatement, Paul.'

Ten minutes later, the night nurse pulled Stephen's clean pyjamas up. She then rolled the dirty linen up and put it into the bucket, which was now empty. She paused for a few seconds and then, not for the first time, glared angrily at Stephen before shouting, 'I'm reporting you to the headmaster in the morning, young man. You have to stop doing this, Stephen. It's not like you're incontinent. As I said to Paul earlier, I could understand if this was an accident; but we both know this wasn't the case on this and other occasions. You are almost 14 years old and therefore you ought to know better. The headmaster needs to know that I'm not putting up with this from you any more, as I've had enough.' An obviously embarrassed Stephen simply put his head down. I have no doubts in my mind that he regretted his actions of that night. The night nurse then looked at me and smiled before saying, 'I'm really sorry that you've had to see this, Paul. If I'd had time, I would have bathed him.' I nodded and replied, 'I have to admit, I have seen better sights during my time at Percy Hedley School.' She smiled once more and then replied, 'I bet you have. Anyway, I'll let you both get some sleep. Goodnight.' She then proceeded to pick the bucket up, turn the light off, and close the door.

After a few minutes, I sat up in bed and said to Stephen, 'Unless you change your ways my friend, you'll end up in a care home, as no one will put up with what you have just done.' Stephen glumly nodded. I followed up by asking, 'You don't want that, do you? You wouldn't be independent at all.' Stephen shook his head and replied, 'No.' I finished the conversation by reiterating, 'You need to think on then. One more thing, when I leave here, I want to be as independent as I can. If you want the same thing for yourself, then you are going totally the wrong way about it. I won't go on about it any more though, but think about what both me and the night nurse have said.' Stephen simply nodded without saying a word. As I went to sleep, I really hoped that he'd indeed take on board what we had said to him.

Luckily for me, after taking advice from the night nurse, Elsie moved Stephen out of my room shortly after the bed messing incident.

Later, I found out that he stopped doing what he did. I was really pleased about that. Whether it had anything to do with 'our chat', I never did find out. But I certainly hope so.

Speaking of night nurses, I'll end this chapter with an incident that happened with a different one at around that time, one who wasn't anywhere near as professional as the individual I've just been talking about.

Bedtimes were fiercely fought battles between the night nurses and the older kids. Teenagers were expected to be in bed by 9.30pm. Can you imagine kids today agreeing to that? Of course they wouldn't. This was not seen as being unfair by the school, but me being me, one night I rebelled because I wanted to watch the end of a TV programme. I was the only person left in the television lounge. This night nurse came in and promptly turned the TV off without even acknowledging me. I wasn't cheeky, but at the same time I wasn't happy, so I said, 'It's not right that a 15-year-old has to be in bed so early.' I then left the room and went to bed.

Once I was in bed, the same night nurse walked across to me and said that I had to go to bed early the following night for being cheeky. The guy I now shared the room with (I think it was Rob) said jokingly, 'Don't forget to set your watch to make sure you tell Paul to go to bed on time.' She then lost her temper and slapped us both on our arms fairly hard. I didn't have a top on so it hurt quite a bit. Nothing was said, but we were both taken aback. Instantly, the individual knew what she'd done. I could tell by the expression on her face that she had regretted her actions. I didn't say a word and simply turned over to go to sleep as she left the room.

Nothing was ever said regarding this incident, though the night nurse was extra nice to us both afterwards, but she never did apologise. I never trusted her from that night until I left school, and therefore I was very wary about what I said to her.

Just like my incidents with the teacher that I mentioned earlier in this book, later I wondered if anything would have been done if we had complained. I'll never know the answer to that, because we didn't. However, with there being two of us perhaps we would have been believed. Maybe that particular night nurse realised this and that was why she was extra nice to us.

Today, what happened that night would have probably resulted in a phone call to Childline. How times change!

Chapter 19

A FEW weeks after Stephen's departure, I was sitting at my desk typing up some homework while listening to a Darlington game at the same time on my radio. I can remember the commentary as if it were yesterday. It went as follows, 'Walsh beats another Bradford defender and shoots. It's a goal! It's 4-0 to the Quakers.' I stopped typing and punched the air in celebration of the goal. I then chanted loudly, 'Walsh, Walsh, Alan, Alan Walsh, he gets the ball he scores a goal, Alan, Alan Walsh!' I know it sounds stupid when I think about it now, but as my mother used to say, 'Boys will be boys!'

Just then, my bedroom door opened and Benny came in without waiting to be invited. I turned away from the radio just in time to hear him ask me, 'Why don't you support a proper team like Newcastle? Rather than a rubbish Division Four one like Darlington?' He then smirked before continuing, 'I mean, come on, Division Four.' To rub it in, he then proceeded to laugh loudly. I smiled and replied, 'I do support a proper team. At least I'm not a glory supporter saying I support a team when I don't even go to watch them play. How many games have you been to this season? Let me guess. Not one.' Benny simply ignored my comments, then walked over to my desk and looked over my shoulder before enquiring, 'Why are you working so late, anyway? You don't get any medals for doing extra homework, you know.' I glanced at him and said, 'It's important to me as I've got my mocks soon. And I want to do well.' Benny shook his head and then smirked before heading over to my bedside table where he started rummaging through my collection of football magazines. I glared at him and shouted, 'Hey! Leave them alone, will you.' He once again ignored me and proceeded to thumb through a copy of *Match*. He rolled it up, put it under his arm and headed quickly towards the door, laughing. To add insult to injury, he revealed, 'This is mine now.' I was furious and yelled, 'Benny. You are a thieving little git.' By this time, he was outside my door smirking and he mocked, 'What are going to do? Run after me? Oh, I forgot, you can't because you are in a wheelchair!' I stared at him angrily. He then continued by stating, 'Thought not because of that, you can't walk. Enjoy your homework, teacher's pet. You probably won't pass your exams anyway.' He then ran off. I shook my head and said to myself out loud, 'We'll see who has the last laugh, Benny boy. Just you wait. It won't be you, that's for sure.'

A week later our school staff, in their ultimate wisdom, arranged a football match against a local comprehensive school. Yours truly was in goal. Here is my recollection of what happened.

CHAPTER 19

The first thing I remembered from the match itself was Benny lunging in for the ball but he missed as the winger from the comprehensive school surged past him as if he wasn't there. Malcolm then scythed him down from behind, showing no mercy whatsoever. The referee, perhaps rather unsurprisingly, only booked him. Maybe he felt sorry for our team, I don't know. The winger got up and proceeded to waste the resulting free kick by simply kicking the ball out of play.

Meanwhile, I patrolled the muddy goalmouth in my wheelchair, wearing a green goalkeeper's jersey and huge gloves.

The next thing I knew was when an able-bodied pupil was clean through our defence. He whacked the ball towards goal. I tried to intercept the shot but it travelled between my flailing hands and nestled in the back of the net. The scorer's team-mates congratulated him (in a somewhat over-the-top manner, so I thought at the time) and the game restarted.

Within seconds, another attack approached and I was on my guard. As the opposition striker was about to pull the trigger, Malcolm pulled his shirt in the area and the opposition player fell to the ground. The striker glared at the referee and yelled, 'Penalty, ref!' The referee pointed to the spot. I tried to psych out the striker, who blasted the ball towards the goal. The next thing I remembered was smack! By sheer luck, the ball bounced off my head, hit the crossbar and went out of play. I was somewhat dazed to say the least. I can, however, remember thinking, 'At least that didn't end up in the net, like most of the other shots they've had.'

The referee and players assembled in a semi-circle around me as the trainer ran on to the pitch and held a bottle of smelling salts under my nose. Once I had fully regained my senses, I excitedly shouted, 'I saved a penalty! I'm just like Phil Owers,' in celebration of the man who was still the Darlington goalkeeper at the time. Malcolm and my team-mates all applauded, which looking back was crazy because the ball hit me! I didn't really save the penalty at all. However, it was a brilliant feeling at the time. A smile comes to my face when I think about it, even after 42 years.

If anyone reading is interested in the score from that day – 24-0 to the comprehensive school. Enough said! Joking apart, it was absolutely fantastic to integrate with able-bodied kids. Looking back as I type this, the staff at Percy Hedley School could and indeed should have done more to encourage this type of thing during my time there. I'm sure that it would have been hugely beneficial to both sets of kids. Unfortunately, it never happened anywhere near enough and the opportunity was lost, which was a real shame in my opinion.

Half an hour after the match, I was in the dressing room, still wearing my goalkeeper's jersey, which was absolutely caked in mud. By this time both Malcolm and Benny were washed and changed. Benny got up to leave as I glared at him and asked, 'Where the hell do you think you're going? We need to have a little chat regarding the magazine you stole from me, my little friend.' Suddenly Benny started to tremble as a smirking Malcolm blocked the doorway with his huge frame. Within a few seconds, he had dragged the by now very frightened Benny into the toilet cubicle. I heard him shouting, 'I'm sorry Paul, I didn't mean it. I won't do it again.' I smirked before shouting back, 'You should have thought about that before you said and did what you did, shouldn't you.'

Without being told, Malcolm then put Benny's head down the toilet and gleefully put his hand in the direction of the flusher. The latter pleaded, 'Let go. I won't do it again, I promise.' Malcolm grinned, then turned and glanced at me (I was still in the dressing room) and asked, 'Shall I flush it, Paul? That would teach him a lesson, wouldn't it?' Knowing that this would be going too far, I shook my head and replied, 'No, he's scared enough. But don't forget the money. Fifty pence he owes me, that's 25 pence for the magazine and the same again for stealing it.' Malcolm smirked, nodded and then righted Benny, spun him round and pinned him with his face pressed against the wall. He then took great pleasure in emptying his pockets and taking out the 50 pence and throwing the rest of the coins on to the tiled floor before releasing him. Smirking, 1 then stared at Benny as if threatening him by stating, 'You can keep the magazine. You've paid for it now. But remember this; don't ever mess with me again as next time you won't get off so lightly.' I paused and then made one final comment, 'I may not be able to walk, as you politely put it last week, but as you can see now, I won't be made a fool of. Don't forget that either.' A still trembling Benny nodded and responded by saying, 'I won't, Paul. I promise.'

Malcolm eventually let go of Benny. Seizing the moment, he collected his money from the floor and escaped from the dressing room, almost colliding with the incoming Elsie, who looked at him with a puzzled expression on her face. She then asked, 'What's wrong with him?' I shrugged my shoulders and replied, 'God knows. You know what he is like.' Elsie nodded, then smiled at Malcolm and said, 'Right, Malcolm, off you go, I need to get our star player into the bath. He's absolutely filthy.' Malcolm smirked at me behind Elsie's back and then left the dressing room. Elsie turned to me and asked, 'Come on Paul, you know that I'm not stupid, what was all that about with Benny? He looked half scared to death.' I acted dumb and replied, 'I haven't got the faintest idea. As I said earlier, you know what he's like, rushing here, there and everywhere.' Elsie gave me a questioning look before responding by saying, 'I suppose you are right.' Later Benny told me that Elsie had asked him about it. He said that he'd been in a rush to get to the television lounge and that was the end of that.

Speaking about being bathed, let me enlighten you with another of my thoughts. It was around this time that I realised the system was seriously flawed. Let me attempt to explain, so please bear with me.

It goes without saying that I recognise that traditionally caring has been a profession mainly for women, going back to Florence Nightingale in the days of the Crimean War. However, not until fairly recently has it been deemed an appropriate career for men.

Nowhere has this been more detrimental to the recipient than in the care and support of young disabled adolescents and men during the years when sexual awakening and exploration occur. This awakening is seen as something quite natural in our non-disabled peers; in fact, it is actively encouraged. Yet in disabled people it was seen as unnatural and actively discouraged. Luckily, this isn't the case now; at least it isn't for me!

Anyway, when active enquiring minds are not challenged in the classroom, the likelihood is they will explore and expand outside of that environment: more human biology was learned in the classrooms by enquiring teenage minds than was ever taught during school hours.

So, my readers, I ask you to place yourselves in some lad's position. Imagine having your intimate parts washed and dried by young ladies who were not much older than you. This is something many other boys could only have fantasies about in their wildest dreams.

The truth with regards to physically disabled teenagers is that could not be further from the reality, for if you exhibited any sign of pleasure let alone becoming aroused, then the wrath of Hades would be brought upon you with full force.

So a coping survival mechanism strategy had to be constructed and be very much mind over matter, where your brain had to train your body not to react.

According to Rob, who this happened to, you train your brain. The head on your shoulders must keep what's in your boxers in check at all times.

Luckily for me, Elsie was in her 40s and not attractive at all, so this didn't happen to me. It must have been truly awful for Rob, without a doubt. Looking back, male carers should have been employed to look after 14- to 16-year-old boys, of that I have no doubt. This would have been much better for the very young female carers as well, some of whom were only months older than us (Julie, for example, was 17) by the time I was ready for leaving school. Many of them, quite understandably, weren't comfortable at all when they had to perform this task.

Thinking about it, when I said earlier that there were no male carers, that wasn't strictly true. Every now and again the council – I think it was the council – would send CVSs (they were originally from the Council for Voluntary Service) to the school, both male and female. Having these young men come into the school had a profound effect on my psyche. They were really good male role models, as well as showing us that there was another way. I suppose in some ways they were the forerunners to the personal assistants that I use today.

I can remember a CVS called David who would often take me to the shops. I was into football sticker books at the time and he helped me to put the pictures into the album that I'd bought. I can remember liking him because he willingly gave me his time, which was great. I can recall being really disappointed when his year was up and he left. In my opinion, if these volunteers were any good, they should have been offered a job. But the school simply replaced them with another body, simply because they didn't have to pay their wages. Being positive, I suppose it was good work experience for them, if they wanted a career in caring. Maybe we put them off; I don't know. But from what I can remember, not many of them actually went into that profession.

Anyway, returning to my friend Benny. Unfortunately, he never did learn his lesson. I will talk more about this in the following chapter.

Chapter 20

A COUPLE of weeks after the match against the local comprehensive school, I was sitting in my room with Malcolm who was looking at one of my football magazines. I paused, smirked and then looked at my friend before asking him, 'Malcolm, do you fancy making a bit of money and having some fun at Benny's expense at the same time?' Malcolm looked up from reading the magazine and gleefully nodded. He then paused and asked, 'How can we do that, Paul?' I smirked again and then said, 'Go and find our little friend.' Malcolm had a puzzled look on his face and asked, 'Why do you want me to get Benny? You don't even like him.' I nodded in agreement and then responded, 'All will be revealed in good time. Trust me.' Malcolm smiled and then carefully put my magazine back in my locker, and smiled before leaving the room.

Ten minutes later, Malcolm entered my room with Benny. I glanced at the latter and said, 'Ah, Benny. Good to see you. I just wanted to let you know that I want to put that unfortunate incident regarding the magazine behind us and to prove there's no hard feelings between you and me from my side anyway, I want to cut you in on a deal that could make us all some money.' An excited Benny nodded eagerly and replied, 'I'm really sorry about the magazine, Paul. As I said, I won't do it again, I promise.' I smiled in his direction prior to saying, 'Oh, I know you are and I also know you won't. Anyway, enough about that; it is in the past now and we need to look to the future. This is what I want you to do ...'

After Benny had left my bedroom, I smirked at Malcolm and revealed, 'He fell for it hook, line and sinker, because he's an absolute idiot. I knew he would. I would have bet my mortgage, if I had one. So, it is game on now and the money will be rolling in very soon.' Malcolm gave me a questioning look and to be honest, looking back now, he seemed very confused. After pausing for a few seconds, he said, 'I really don't understand at all, Paul. What are you up to?' I smiled in his direction and stated, 'Don't worry about it, Malcolm. You don't need to. All you need to know is that we'll be long gone by the time the headmaster finds out what's happened.'

The following evening, there was a queue of disabled children waiting outside an office door which wasn't in use after school lessons were finished. Benny walked down the queue and took ten pence from each child. He then addressed the children, almost like a sergeant major (he was obviously loving the role of having power over the children) and said, 'Don't forget, boys and girls, you are only allowed three minutes each on the phone. I'll knock on the door when your time is up. Make sure you say your "goodbyes" and then put the phone down straight away as we are really tight for time.' Benny then glanced at a girl who walked with a limp and said, 'Right, Michelle [not her real name], you are first.' He then opened the office door and the girl eagerly hobbled in.

Around the corner from the office, out of sight of Benny, Malcolm and I watched the proceedings with great interest. I looked at him and said, 'Hmm; there's 12 people in the queue. That's £1.20. Not bad at all for the first time we have done this.' Malcolm smirked and piped up, 'Have you seen him bossing the kids around? He is really enjoying himself.' I smirked then nodded before stating, 'I know he is a sad little cretin. But as long as we get the money, I'm not really bothered to be honest.'

Later in the evening, Malcolm and I were sitting at my bedside table playing cards when Benny entered and handed over some coins to Malcolm, who by this time, had already thrown his three card brag hand in and said, 'You beat me again. I'm glad we weren't playing for money.' Malcolm then counted the money Benny had given him and announced, 'There's only 80 pence here, Paul. By my count, we are 40 pence short. He's ripped you off.' On hearing Malcolm's comment, Benny went white with fear. He tried his best to hold his nerve, but couldn't. I shook my head and then glared at Benny before enquiring, 'Are you sure only eight kids used the office phone?' Benny nodded and replied, 'Yes, Paul. Honest. I wouldn't lie to you. Not after what happened last time.' I stared at him and shouted, 'I know you aren't telling me the truth yet again because a little bird told me there were 12 kids wanting to use the phone! First you thieve from me and then when I give you a second chance, you try and rob me blind. You are a sneaky little shit.' I then smirked in Malcolm's direction and stated, 'It looks like our little friend didn't learn his lesson from last time. Perhaps he needs a refresher course!' I then shook my head and then smirked again before continuing, 'I don't know, Malcolm, some people just never learn.' Malcolm smiled and then nodded in agreement.

I then said to my friend, 'Tip him upside down, and let's see what drops out of his pockets. I bet 40 pence ends up on my carpet.' Fortunately for Benny, before Malcolm could do anything to him, he suddenly started to cry and took the aforementioned 40 pence from his trouser pocket and handed it over to the ever-willing Malcolm. I smiled and stated, 'That's better, you scheming little git. Next time don't waste your time trying to rip me off. You simply aren't clever enough. I would have thought you'd have learned that from our last experience. But obviously not.' Benny nervously nodded and then meekly replied, 'I won't Paul, I promise.' I looked at him and said, 'Your empty promises don't mean anything to me at all to be honest, Benny.' I then glanced at Malcolm and said, 'Give him 20 pence, matey. Though thinking about it again, after he's tried to tear my eyes out, he doesn't really deserve it. But unlike him, I keep my promises.' Malcolm did what he was asked.

All the time I continued to glare at Benny. Eventually, I yelled, 'Now get out and don't forget what I've said. One other thing before you go, if you ever try to con me again, I'll get Malcolm to put your head down the toilet and flush it. Do you understand?' Benny nodded and replied, 'Yes Paul.' Not surprisingly after what had happened, he then beat a hasty retreat. I have to admit, I did smirk when I saw his red face as he left. After Benny had gone, Malcolm looked at me and asked, 'You wouldn't really do that, would you?' I shook my head and replied, 'Of course not. I stopped you from doing it after the football match, didn't I? The thing is Benny doesn't know that.'

After a few seconds, I looked at Malcolm and said, 'You take 40 pence for yourself and can you please put the rest into my wallet. It will come in handy for when I play cards later on tonight.' After he'd done what I'd asked, he looked at me with a puzzled look on his face and enquired, 'Do you know when you said the other day we'd be long gone by the time the headmaster finds out? How? I don't understand. I've wracked my brain about it but I honestly don't know what you were on about.' I smirked before responding by revealing, 'It is easy. The school phone bill comes in every six months. The next one is due in September. We both will have left school by then.' Malcolm paused for a few seconds and then nodded in partial understanding. I then continued, 'Plus, due to the way that I planned it, all the kids think it is Benny's little racket. With this in mind, when he comes back from his summer holiday, he'll be in the shit with the headmaster, big time. The only sad thing for me is that we won't be here to see it. As that would have been great fun. Obviously, if we had been here, he would have tried to blame us, but we'd have simply said that we didn't know what he was on about. All the kids who used the phone would have backed that story up, so the headmaster wouldn't have believed him.'

Malcolm smirked as my plan finally sank into his head. He simply remarked, 'You are very clever, Paul. Your plan is brilliant.' Again I smirked as I said, 'Thanks. I think it is foolproof. In addition, it is a good little money-maker, especially if we do it a few more times before we leave.' Malcolm nodded and then smiled. I concluded, 'That little shit will rue the day he bullied and stole from me. No one will ever get away with that where I'm concerned; now or in the future. Hopefully it'll teach him a lesson in life, though somehow I doubt it as people like that never change. He'll probably end up in borstal one day.'

Interestingly, several years later, I did find out that Benny had indeed spent time inside, which was a shame, but on the other hand you have to take responsibility for your own actions.

Chapter 21

IN MY last year at Percy Hedley I really started to take a lot more notice how the staff ran the care side of things. It was certainly interesting to survey this and looking back, they wouldn't have got away with things today that they did back then.

Many of the housemothers simply sat in the TV lounge smoking and reading newspapers in between the end of tea and the start of bath time. It only dawned on me, as I took a far greater interest, that they didn't actually know where some of the kids were that they were responsible for, or far more importantly, what they were up to. Malcolm for example used to take me to the shops (just to get out of the school for a while) and on many occasions neither of us were ever missed. In case you are wondering, I can honestly say that the pair of us always behaved ourselves while we were away from the school premises.

That aside, thinking about this now, we got away with this far too easily and in theory we could have been on a train to London by the time we probably would have been missed.

CHAPTER 21

I have to say, in fairness to Elsie, that she was a good housemother and apart from me sneaking to the shops on the odd occasion, she always knew where I was. However, I quickly noticed that some of the other housemothers weren't as good as her, and I often wondered about why they didn't interact and do things to stimulate their kids, especially the younger ones, many of whom just sat bored out of their heads watching rubbish that happened to be on the television. Surely, it would have made far more sense rather than simply sitting and gossiping – with cigarettes hanging from their mouths – with one another. On seeing this several times per week, a question popped into my head: What stopped them from taking the kids out for a walk or playing board games with them, like the very kind Mr O'Dowd did with me several years earlier? This would have been easy to do and yet in all my time at Percy Hedley School, I didn't see this happen once as far as I can remember. As a result, the kids ended up vegetating in front of the television. To be fair the younger kids did have Cubs once a week, which I'm sure was very stimulating and indeed enjoyable for them, but apart from that, there was very little for them to do after lessons had finished and they'd had their tea.

In between tea finishing and the start of bath time, if memory serves me right, there was just over an hour, so, in my opinion there was nothing to stop these care staff from doing something more entertaining with the children in their care. Even now when I think back to those times, I wonder why they didn't do more in that hour or so. Maybe they just couldn't be bothered, I don't know. One thing I do know was that I personally tried to keep away from the TV lounge during that hour (or if I did go in there, I didn't stay long, though long enough to see that nothing had changed), simply because you could hardly see what was in front of you because of the cigarette smoke billowing around the room! After the housemothers had left to start bathing the kids, the smell every late afternoon was unreal and this can't have been good for the health of the children left in there and having to put up with that stench. It goes without saying that this wouldn't happen today because smoking in the workplace isn't allowed. However, it shouldn't have happened then either. Of that, there's no doubt in my opinion.

In addition to the above, some of the kids with learning difficulties simply ran wild and their housemothers were blissfully smoking in the TV room totally unaware of what was going on.

I can remember one occasion when some of the kids with learning difficulties arranged a fight with some local youths in the churchyard, which was situated next door to the school. The boys from our school were big lads, and they were simply too strong for their counterparts and won the battle easily. Not one of them had a mark on them, which was amazing. Unfortunately, the same couldn't be said of the local youths! I was surprised that their parents didn't come to our school to complain. But none did. I presume that the able-bodied kids hadn't told them what had gone on (probably because getting beaten up by a load of disabled kids wouldn't have done their street credibility any good at all), otherwise I think some of them would have paid the school a visit! The only reason I found out about the fight was because Malcolm gleefully told me all about it, in great detail. Not for the first time, the housemothers who were responsible for these children didn't have a clue what had happened, which looking back, I find totally unbelievable as ten to 12 children with learning difficulties were missing for at least an hour without their knowledge.

During my nine years at Percy Hedley School there were many other incidents such as this, but I don't want this to be a one-sided point of view. As I've mentioned many times in this book, people like Elsie were very good carers and were mostly on top of things. In other words, staff like her did actually 'care' for the children in their charge. I personally saw this for myself. However, sadly, some of the other staff weren't like that and therefore, the kids in their care (I use that term very loosely where these individuals are concerned) simply got away with murder.

Another of my concerns was that there was only ONE night nurse to look after all the boys. There was another to look after the girls who, as I mentioned earlier, resided in a different part of the school.

Anyway, as I got older, I began to wonder, 'If there's a fire, or some other kind of emergency, how would this ONE night nurse get all the kids, many of whom were severely disabled, out of the building?' It would have been impossible. Maybe this was done to keep costs down (costs shouldn't have come into it), I don't know, but it certainly wouldn't be allowed today, that's for sure; as it was an accident waiting to happen. Luckily it didn't while I was there.

In my last year at Percy Hedley School I found out for myself how hard a job it was to care for all these children when Malcolm, Rob, his friend and I were tasked with putting all the kids to bed because the night nurse who was on duty was at the staff Christmas party and obviously didn't want to leave the festivities! You couldn't script it, could you? Or, maybe I could!

Anyway, Rob and I instructed Malcolm and the other lad what to do, step by step. We put each age group to bed separately. Some of the kids wouldn't tell us which bed they slept in, so I said, 'Bung him in any bed.' Funnily enough, once I said that they quickly revealed which bed was theirs. I have to admit, I did find their antics highly amusing.

The four of us put every kid to bed. It took us absolutely ages, as some of them played up by, for example, pretending to want to go to the toilet when they had just been, but overall, I have to say, it was a job well done.

Looking back, we shouldn't have been expected to do this job as cover night nurses could and indeed should have been hired, and indeed shown the ropes long before the party. Unfortunately, this wasn't done and the four of us were simply expected to put the kids to bed as had been the case every year previously. We didn't do it every year, different senior kids did it for each party, but when we were the oldest pupils we were expected to do it. A simple question sprang to mind then and it is still relevant today. What would have happened if one of the kids in our care, or indeed any other senior's, had been accidentally dropped or had some kind of health problem? It wouldn't have been any use going for the night nurse who was 'on duty' because she'd been drinking at the party! I would have loved to have been a fly on the wall if/when a senior staff member would have had to explain to a child's parents why the night staff were at a party drinking alcohol and four final-year pupils had been instructed to put their loved one to bed, totally unsupervised. It would certainly have been an interesting conversation Luckily, this didn't happen as Rob and I ensured that there were no mishaps. There weren't any in previous years either. However, senior students shouldn't have been put in that position in the first place.

Chapter 22

OVER THE years, in secondary our class were taken away for five days for a holiday.

We went to places like Whitby and Edinburgh. The latter still holds fond memories for me as Mr O'Dowd pushed me around the Botanical Gardens and up Princes Street. The trip around the gardens was particularly enjoyable as I was amazed how many names of flowers and plants he knew. Looking back, I was so lucky to have that man as my mentor. I honestly believe that he helped me become the person I am today.

Now to simply the worst trip I ever went on. Let me explain.

A representative from a local university (that shall remain nameless) contacted the school and the result of that conversation was that someone from Percy Hedley School, in their ultimate wisdom, thought it would be a good idea to allow a group of students to take around a dozen disabled pupils out into the wilds of nowhere for a weekend.

No teachers or care staff from the school went with us, which thinking about it now, should never have been allowed and looking back was disgraceful. So off we went with cans of beans and more cans of beer. Eventually, we ended up in a converted barn on the edge of Holy Island. To this day I am unsure who was responsible for whom. The whole weekend passed in a drunken haze.

That in itself would not have been so bad had not a certain Kevin – I shall not say his full name – not been scared of the dark and convinced Rob to go and sit outside the privy while he had a pee. Unfortunately for him he neglected to put his wheelchair brakes on, so while he was merrily peeing, Rob rolled over a six-foot high step, landing on his face. He awoke hours later lying on the barn floor dazed, not knowing who he was or where he was. His face resembled Frankenstein's monster's ugly brother!

The drunken students did not deem it necessary to call an ambulance. If he hadn't been stinking drunk (as was I along with all the other kids and 'carers') I swear he could have been killed that night.

Another quite bad thing that happened that weekend was two very drunken students trying to have sex in the same room I was trying to sleep.

The guy couldn't manage it and the girl got frustrated. The girl got off the top of the lad, still naked, came over to my bed and asked, 'Do you fancy a bit of fun?' It goes without saying that despite being drunk, I declined the offer! I was 16 at the time, so I could have done it legally, but I just couldn't, as I didn't fancy her one bit. After being turned down, she paused for a few seconds. She then blurted out, 'Your loss,' before storming off. I smirked as she walked away, frustrated to say the least! Personally, I found the whole scenario highly amusing and still do to this day.

Needless to say, on our return, the experiment of students taking disabled children away was quickly shelved by the school once the extent of the horror was told. I think the state of Rob's face and hands told the whole story. I kept my incident quiet, much to the girl's relief. To her credit, the day afterwards, she did apologise to me. I accepted her apology and everything was forgotten.

If I recall correctly, my mother threatened to take the story regarding Rob and no one from the school being in attendance to the local press. She must have been talked out of it by a staff member from Percy Hedley because they were never contacted.

Many years later I told her about my incident with that girl. Quite naturally, she was appalled that a 'carer' had come on to someone she was supposed to be looking after. She said that if I'd told her at the time, she would have taken it further, without a doubt. Me being me, I simply put it down to experience and moved on with my life. I have to admit, until I started to write this book, I hadn't given this incident another thought since the day I told my mother. So it didn't affect me at all.

As with many of the other incidents which occurred during my time at Percy Hedley, a trip like that would never have been sanctioned today and it shouldn't have been then either.

Whoever made the decision to allow the weekend away to go ahead without any staff from the school attending, must have been crazy to say the least. Rob could have been quite easily killed due to his fall, as well as being left on the floor with concussion with no treatment offered. When I asked a guy why an ambulance wasn't called, he simply stated, 'None of us even thought about that to be honest.' That answer summed up better than anything why this trip shouldn't have been allowed to happen. In addition, looking back, the incident with the girl also wasn't right, although I find it amusing in one way, but thinking about it another, it was certainly a breach of trust; one that shouldn't have happened. In addition, trying to have sex with that male student in the same room as I was trying to sleep in wasn't good either!

Luckily, by hook or by crook, there was no long-term damage, but that was no thanks to those drunken students, or the school for that matter.

I have to say this was the only 'nightmare' trip I went on. As I've mentioned previously, all the others were truly memorable, for the right reasons.

Chapter 23

JUST BEFORE I left school, I was asked by the headmaster to go over the road to the Percy Hedley Work Centre on work experience.

However, prior to that, something else regarding 'work' happened that I feel I must mention. So here goes.

One day, Rob and I went to see the careers advisor. We both knew it would be a complete waste of time because boys with such 'severe disabilities' (his words, not ours) were destined to end up in the day centre across the road. Residential college for two years prior was also an option. I can remember thinking, 'Maybe this guy is on commission for getting as many young adults as possible to throw their lives down the drain and make more money for the Percy Hedley Foundation in the process by getting school leavers to go to the work centre after they finished their college courses.' At that time in my life, neither option was for me as I wanted to get out into the world and if possible find a job, then return to education at a later date.

Within the first minute of the interview, the pair of us quickly realised he was never going to help us achieve our goals and was only too keen for us both to be dumped in the work centre (maybe my assumption, albeit tongue in cheek, was correct and he was on commission). With this in mind, I told him I wanted to be an astronaut and be the first disabled person on the moon whereas Rob opted for a fireman. Not surprisingly, we were both thrown out of the office with a flea in our ears. I can still remember the words 'Grow up!' as the pair of us left the room. I have to admit, his face was a picture!

Getting back to the work centre, I explained to the headmaster when I visited his office one morning in no uncertain terms that I had no intention of spending the rest of my life over there as I wanted to get out into the wide world and experience life, rather than become institutionalised. Nevertheless, after some arm-twisting and against my better judgement, I agreed to go there for half a day for four weeks. Looking back, I wished I hadn't wasted 16 hours of my life that I'll never get back. Here's what happened.

Luckily, Rob was over there for the same four weeks as me, so at least I knew someone. Every Friday morning the pair of us would spend mind-numbing time putting toothbrushes and toothpaste into bigger boxes from an already pre-packed smaller box! My first question to the supervisor was, 'Why are we doing this? These are already packed.' He replied, 'It isn't up to you to question how things are done here.' I simply shook my head as we were doing work that had already been completed, probably by a machine! What a total waste of time for the poor souls who were trapped there and were expected to do this boring, and more importantly, pointless 'job' day in and day out, for the rest of their lives. All I could think was, 'I'm far, far better than this.' Doing this 'job' made me even more determined not to end up there. Luckily I didn't, but it was only down to my sheer determination not to throw my life down the toilet that I didn't. Luckily my mother supported me all the way regarding this, so it would never have happened in a million years.

We were both absolutely useless at this 'job' and more toothbrushes ended up down our wheelchairs! This meant for years afterwards, our families and neighbours never went short of dental hygiene equipment; I ended up with hundreds of items by the time the four weeks was up! Our bathroom cupboard at home was full to overflowing which I found highly amusing. That was the only good bit! Joking apart, the whole exercise was a complete waste of both their and more importantly our time. Even before going there, I knew that would have been the case. Looking back, I would rather have watched paint dry for 16 hours than go to that place! In fairness, it would probably have been more exciting!

Anyway, after my month was up, the headmaster called me into his office and asked me what I thought of life at the work centre. I told him in no uncertain terms what I thought. I sat back expecting a severe telling-off. However, I was surprised and somewhat unnerved at what happened next. After a few seconds, he just smiled. Then the bombshell was delivered. He said, 'Paul, exactly, and if you do not pull your finger out that is your future. You need a plan of what you want to do with your life.' I responded by saying, 'I have one, I intend to experience the world, try to find some kind of work and return to education later. I was only winding the careers advisor up about wanting to be an astronaut.' However, despite me having a sensible answer for him, those words had a shocking effect on me and I did pull my finger out, and on leaving the headmaster's office that day I was even more determined to succeed in life and never end up in a place like that. I had no intention of going there anyway but that was the final kick up the backside that 100 per cent ensured that I didn't.

Many years later, Rob informed me in one of our many telephone conversations, that the headmaster had said exactly the same thing to him, almost word for word. He must have said the same thing to every young person who'd said what we had. If going over there was meant to be a shock tactic, it certainly worked, as neither of us ended up going to the work centre and we both ended up having very productive working lives.

Thinking about it all these years later, even though I had very little education from Percy Hedley School, the lesson the headmaster gave me during that four weeks and the subsequent conversation we had, I will never forget and I will be for ever grateful to him for that.

Finally, I feel that I must conclude this chapter with a telephone conversation regarding that so-called careers advisor that I had with Rob a couple of years ago.

We both agreed that we would love to meet him now and give him the finger, say to him, 'Look what we have both achieved after being written off by you. We both went on to have interesting and productive careers, own our own homes and have meaningful, loving relationships.' The man didn't have any options apart from the work centre and further education, something that I'll touch on in more detail later. No jobs were mentioned at all. There was no feeling or any real interest from him, just a prepared script, which he never diverted from. In reality, he was picking up money for old rope and the school was getting a box ticked, which was morally wrong, but unfortunately was a sign of those times: disabled people were simply written off.

To this day I feel more could and indeed should have been done, if more effort had been put in by that 'careers advisor' (I use that term very lightly). In fairness to him, some of it was the times we grew up in, but to this day I feel that he could have done a hell of a lot more for intelligent young adults like Rob and I rather than take the easy option. If you delve into this further, how many disabled young people were simply dumped in the work centre when if supported, they could have offered a lot more to society? (It is similar to Hitler's ideas regarding the disabled and we all know how that ended up.) I honestly dread to think.

At that time it was easier to keep disabled people out of sight and away from everyday life and for God's sake stop them from breeding! However, yet again, that's a story for another day. It is worrying and indeed quite upsetting to think how many lives could and maybe should have been different, if help/support had been given at the right time. Unfortunately, more often than not, this didn't happen and disabled young adults ended up being dumped in residential care, because it was the easy option for society at that time.

As Rob said during our telephone conversation, 'You may beat us, bruise us, but you will never break us.' I certainly couldn't argue there! Luckily, the pair of us had two things that helped us: sheer determination to ensure that we would go on to have fulfilling lives and supportive parents (in my case one) who always had our back; if that hadn't been the case, it could have been oh so different. This is indeed a scary thought to end this chapter on!

Chapter 24

SHORTLY AFTER the infamous stint at the work centre, I was getting ready to embark on the next part of my life; as it was almost time for me to leave Percy Hedley School and head out into the big, wide world. In many ways, I'd been sheltered from that world for the nine years I'd been away from home. With this in mind, it was with slight trepidation, as I was taking this huge step; however, even at such a young age, I knew in my own mind that I'd make a success of my life, as I was absolutely determined to ensure that I did so, if only to prove my father wrong.

Anyway, the day before it was time for me to leave, Malcolm was helping me to sort my personal effects out.

I watched him as he took down my Athena 'Tennis Girl' poster. I glanced at the poster then at him and said, 'It's yours now, Malcolm.' My friend smiled excitedly and replied, 'Really? Can I put it on my bedroom wall when I go to the work centre?' I nodded and responded by stating, 'Yeah, of course you can. As I said, it is yours now, so you can do what you want with it.' Malcolm stopped what he was doing, paused for a few seconds and said, 'I wish you were coming with me, Paul.' I smiled at him and commented, 'I have to go and make my own way in life. Therefore, going to the work centre isn't part of my plan. It's just not the place for me.' Malcolm paused for a few seconds, nodded and then asked, 'So, what are you going to do?' I shrugged my shoulders and then said, 'I don't quite know yet, mate. Hopefully, I'll get a job. That's my plan anyway. Eventually, I'll go to college; but now isn't the time for that.' Malcolm smiled and then said, 'I'll miss you, as you've been a really good friend to me over the years.' I smiled and said, 'I'll miss you too, my friend. We certainly made a good team; that's for sure.' Malcolm then hugged me. I genuinely felt bad about leaving him, but in my heart of hearts I knew that I had to follow my gut feeling and strive to have the best life I could and going to the work centre certainly wouldn't help me achieve my aims.

The following morning, I was looking at the CSE results board which was situated in the corridor when the headmaster appeared behind me and put his hand on my shoulder. He smiled and said, 'That's right, Paul. Four passes. Well done. Mrs Moore and Mr O'Dowd both said to me that you worked really hard. Like I've always preached to the children here, that pays off and it certainly did with you.' I glanced at the headmaster and said, 'Many thanks for those kind words. It's just a shame there were only four of us who took any exams.' He paused and then nodded before stating, 'I agree. But four is better than none, Paul. We have to start somewhere and you and the three others have helped us along the road that hopefully one day will lead to more children being able to take exams.' I nodded and replied, 'I guess so. Thank you for those kind words.' I could have commented on the standard of education offered at the school. However, I quickly decided that particular day wasn't the one to have that kind of conversation. One final comment regarding the headmaster: he was always very kind to me and like Mr O'Dowd, he was an excellent chess player; once, after many attempts, I did eventually beat him, but only when I became a pretty good player. Beating him gave me as much pleasure as when I overcame Mr O'Dowd for the first time.

Later that day, Agnes came to pick me up to take me home, for the very last time.

In the school car park, the taxi driver stowed my suitcase in the boot of his car as Agnes very kindly waited for me to finish talking to Malcolm, who was standing next to me. I had a plastic carrier bag in my hand. I glanced at my friend and said, 'Why not come and see me sometime? You will always be very welcome.' I then handed him the carrier bag, smirked and said, 'Anyway, have a look in this bag, my friend.' Malcolm smiled and then gleefully put his hand into the bag and pulled out four cans of lager. He smiled once more at me and enquired, 'Are these for me, Paul?' I nodded and responded by saying, 'Yeah. But make sure that you hide them in a better place than you did the last time we bought cans. The top of the wardrobe isn't a very good idea.' We both laughed at the shared memory. I glanced at him and continued, 'And make sure you get yourself out a bit more instead of spending all your time cooped up indoors. Whitley Bay's just up the road and I know you like it there.' Malcolm smiled before replying by stating, 'I'll try, Paul. Honest I will.' He then gave me a farewell bearhug.

Unfortunately, after leaving school, I didn't see as much of him as I would have liked, which was a real shame. The last I heard, he ended up not going to the work centre after all and went home. That is probably why we lost touch. On several occasions later in life, I tried to find him on social media, but without success.) One final thing about him, he was a really good friend to me during my whole time at Percy Hedley School, through both the good times and the bad, and I never forgot him for that.

Finally, I thought that it would be a good idea to finish this chapter by saying a few words and indeed give my thoughts on Percy Hedley School. So here goes.

Firstly, I have to say most of the staff at the school, especially Lynn Birrell, Alison Carlisle and later Gillian Miller, certainly made me more independent and I'll always be grateful to them for that. As you will recall, when I first went there, I could hardly string two words together, nor could I sit up without being propped up with cushions. This certainly wasn't the case when I left, which was a massive improvement, without doubt.

Without their help and indeed patience, I wouldn't be where I am today.

As I've mentioned a few times already, I'm of the impression that the educational part of the school could have been a lot better. Having children with learning difficulties in the same class as physically disabled ones certainly didn't work. I'm really pleased to hear that this is no longer the case, which is great. However, this was a great frustration for me while I was there as I feel that if the teachers could have spent more time with students like Rob and I, instead of trying to keep children with far fewer capabilities entertained, I would have come out with a lot more than four CSEs. I can't stress enough that this certainly wasn't the teachers' fault; it was the system. It was flawed. This was certainly unfortunate in our case. Another huge gripe of mine was being made to do pottery and art. In my humble opinion, in my case, this was a complete and utter waste of my time and indeed the teacher's as it would have been far more beneficial for me to do maths or English, rather than get clarted up to the eyeballs with clay. This still bugs me to this day.

Looking back, with some exceptions, a lot of the staff did a brilliant job. Mr O'Dowd and Mrs Moore, in my opinion, excelled and left an indelible mark on my life for which I'll be eternally grateful for as without their help and indeed their confidence in my abilities, once again, I wouldn't be where I am today. They worked in extremely trying circumstances and yet still got four children through their CSEs. This to me was a magnificent achievement that shouldn't ever be underestimated by anyone.

Unfortunately, some staff will be remembered by me for entirely the wrong reasons. Thinking about this as I'm sitting here typing away, there's good and bad in all walks of life. While certain things that happened to me while I was there proved to be extremely difficult, in some ways they made me the man I am today. Though those who treated me badly have left a negative imprint on my memory.

When I wrote *Flipper's Side*, I left a lot of the bad things regarding my education out. Maybe I wasn't ready to reveal all back in 2000, I don't know. However, in this book I've tried to be honest regarding this and I think I have been. Some of the conversations regarding my school days aren't word-for-word correct, but the content is and that in my opinion is the most important thing. As I've mentioned throughout this story, some names have been changed as well. I felt this was only fair to the children concerned.

One final thing that I have to say, Elsie Ferguson was a brilliant housemother and certainly looked after the children in her care really well. That was because she actually 'cared' which, in my opinion, made a huge difference to our lives. I was lucky that I was allocated her to look after me, as some of the other housemothers certainly weren't up to her standards.

Looking back over my time at Percy Hedley School, yes, I had problems there and things happened that shouldn't have; I certainly left the place a lot better off than I was the first day I was pushed through the doors. So from a personal point of view, I'm certainly glad that my mother made the very brave decision to send me there. I'll be for ever grateful to her for that.

Chapter 25

A FEW weeks after I'd left school, I was sitting in the living room with my father when my mother came in from work.

As she put her coat on the back of the sofa, she glanced at us both and said, 'So what have you two lazy buggers been up to today?' My father answered first and responded by saying, 'I've had a couple of hours down at the allotment. I've left you some vegetables in the kitchen.' My mother then nudged me on the shoulder and asked, 'And you – I thought you were applying to go to college?' I looked to her and said, 'I don't feel ready for that yet, mam. I've been away from home for nine years. I will go to college, I promise. But I'm going to try and get a job first.' I showed her the jobs page from the *Northern Echo* newspaper with several vacancies circled. My father glared at me and yelled, 'A bloody job! I can't get one so what makes you think you can?' I paused and tried my utmost to stay calm and replied, 'Qualifications, Dad. I have four decent CSEs now.' His face went bright red as he glared at my mother and shouted, 'Alice! Did you hear what he just said? There are nearly three million people unemployed, so how the hell can he expect to get a job? Four CSEs won't make any difference whatsoever.' Like me, my mother stayed calm and responded by stating, 'Well, maybe he can get a job. I know my heart was set on him going to college straight away but he has to make his own decisions now. Who knows, the qualifications may help, they certainly won't do any harm, will they?' My father angrily shook his head and at the top of his voice exclaimed, 'He's a bloody idiot. And you are no better, encouraging him with his daft ideas. He'll never get a job, live on his own or get married. We'll be stuck with him for ever, leaching off us.'

By this time, despite my best efforts to stay calm, I was frustrated to say the least and I said angrily, 'We'll see. You said I wouldn't sit up, I did, you said I wouldn't talk, I did. I proved you wrong then, and I will again. Just you see.' Once again, he shook his head and glared at my mother before shouting, 'If he thinks he can just sponge off me for the rest of his life, he's got another thing coming. Because, I'll tell you right now, I'm not bloody well having it.' Like me, by this stage, she had lost her patience and yelled, 'You're a fine one to talk about sponging with the amount of times you are on the sick and sponge out of my wages. That's how you lost your last job, because you were never there. It wouldn't be so bad if you were really sick, but you're not. You are just bone idle and don't want work and you never have. If you had Paul's determination, you'd never be out of work. Instead you are content to sit on your fat arse, just like you have for most of your life.' Those words were like a red rag to a bull to my father (they must have struck a chord as to be honest, I thought he was going to have a heart attack), and again at the top of his voice he preached, 'At least I do some bloody work. He's nothing but a …' My mother wasn't having any of it as by now she was fuming. She interrupted him mid-sentence and even louder than he had shouted, she enquired, 'Nowt but a what?' Without saying another word, my father angrily got up, left the room and slammed the door behind him. I honestly thought the door was going to come off its hinges! My mother glared at the door and shouted, 'Yes, go on, run away when you hear the truth, just like you have all your life. You are the failure, Norman, not Paul.'

After calming down, I looked at my mother and revealed, 'At least I won't have to see very much of the miserable git tomorrow with me going to Uncle Alan's to help him with his CB radio.' She nodded and then replied, 'Ah. Yes, I'd forgotten about that. You should have a good time with him. At least he's not a miserable git.' She then smirked.

Please note, as with many of the conversations in this book, the above one isn't word-for-word correct. However, the facts are.

The following morning, Uncle Alan was sitting at my kitchen table. He put his empty mug into the sink, looked at me and asked, 'Are you ready to go, son? I can't wait to get my new CB working.' I smiled at him and said, 'Yes, I'm ready when you are.' Just then, my father entered the room carrying a basket full of pigeons and glanced at Alan before asking, 'On your way to Northallerton, would you mind releasing these for me? I'll get the basket back when you bring Paul home.' My uncle was hesitant and revealed, 'I've only just cleaned my car out, Norman. I'm not sure.' I looked towards him and said, 'Oh, go on Uncle Alan, it's on our way. Plus, if you put some newspapers in your boot first, there won't be as much mess as you'll be able to roll them up and put them in the bin when you get back.' I have to say, my father was rather taken aback when he heard me plead on his behalf. After a few seconds, Alan smiled and stated, 'Yes, I suppose you are right, Paul. I could hoover up any excess mess in the car boot again tonight. The newspapers will certainly make that job easier, though.' My father nodded and said, 'Thanks Alan, I really appreciate this.' Alan glanced at him and said, 'Don't thank me. Thank your son; he talked me into doing this for you.' My father paused for a few seconds then said quietly, 'Thanks Paul.' I smiled and replied, 'No worries.'

A few minutes later, I was sitting in the front seat of my uncle's bright-yellow Ford Escort. From his seat next to me, he commented, 'It's not like you to want to help your dad out like that. What are you up to?' I smirked and revealed, 'You are quite right. I don't.' Alan gave me a questioning look and asked, 'What do you mean? We've got his stinking pigeons in the boot of my car.' Again I smirked in his direction and said, 'I know, he thinks we are going to let them go just outside Northallerton. However, if we wait a bit, say 20 minutes, then let them off just outside Darlington, they'll get back to his loft in no time, and he'll think he has championship-winning birds. Trust me, it will be really funny because he'll never know and will brag to all and sundry about it.' Alan laughed loudly before exclaiming, 'Brilliant! Come on, let's go for a quick beer, then we'll let his pigeons off in the park across town.' I nodded in agreement before saying, 'That sounds like a plan.' Alan smirked and said, 'I'd love to see his face if he found out.' I nodded before responding, 'So would I. I might tell him one day, but on the other hand, I might not.' Alan smiled and said, 'Don't worry, your secret is safe with me.' I patted him on the shoulder and commented, 'I know I can trust you, Uncle Alan.'

Later that afternoon, I was sitting at the kitchen table having a cup of tea with my mother. I told her the story about the pigeons and finished by revealing, 'So we let them off in the park at the other side of Darlington.' Just then we heard the front door open. My mother smiled and said, 'Shhh. We don't want him to overhear us talking about it.'

Less than a minute later, my smiling father entered the kitchen. He glanced at us both and almost childlike he revealed, 'You never guess what? My birds made it back from Northallerton in four minutes from the time you let them off! It looks like I'll do well in the big race at the weekend. I knew that I had championship-winning birds on my hands. The other pigeon lads were laughing at me when I was telling them. They won't be when I win the big race on Saturday.' My mother looked at him and replied, 'That's really great, Norman. I'm really pleased for you. You are right, they won't be laughing then.' My father smiled again (I have to admit, I found this really eerie as he seldom did it) and said, 'Yeah, I'm over the moon. I'm just off to the toilet.' My mother nodded and responded by saying, 'Hurry up. Your tea won't be long.' My father, still smiling, nodded as he left the room.

After the coast was clear, I looked at my mother and smirked before remarking, 'It worked a treat. He is a bloody idiot.' She nodded in agreement and said, 'That certainly got him back for last night, didn't i?' I smirked again and finished the conversation by making this comment, 'Too right! Championship-winning birds my arse. And the funny thing is his so-called mates will be laughing their caps off when they come in two or three hours behind the rest on Saturday. I have to say, it serves him right.'

I never did tell my dad what happened that day. However, my mother, Uncle Alan and I had many, many laughs, even years later, when we talked about it.

Chapter 26

A COUPLE of weeks after fooling my father about his pigeons, I was out at a pub with Ian and his future wife Lynn. We were celebrating my friend getting his job with the Ministry of Defence, where he works to this day. However, he's a manager now.

Anyway, my lager glass was empty, so Ian smirked and then asked, 'I suppose you want another?' I smiled and responded by saying, 'Is the Pope Catholic, my friend?' Ian then glanced at Lynn and enquired, 'Same again?' Lynn smiled and then nodded her head and replied, 'Yes please.' Ian smiled back at his girlfriend, then got up and headed towards the bar, leaving me with Lynn.

Shortly after, a man approached our table, pint in hand. He glanced at me and said, 'I've seen you before at the football. You're Paul, aren't you?' I nodded and then said, 'Yes, I'm Paul. I've seen you there too. You stand in the East Stand Paddock if my memory serves me right.' He smiled and then revealed, 'Yes, that's right. I do. My name's Tom [not his real name]. I'm the chairman of Darlington Supporters' Club. Mind if I join you?' I gestured towards one of the empty chairs before saying, 'Take a seat, Tom.' Tom smiled and then sat down as Ian returned carrying a tray of drinks.

I glanced at Tom and revealed, 'We're just out celebrating Ian's new job at the MoD. He only found out he'd got it this morning.' Tom smiled at Ian and then said, 'Congratulations Ian.' Ian, who by now was sitting at the table, smiled before saying, 'Thanks Tom. I'm really pleased, as I know how hard it is to get a job these days.' Tom then glanced at me and asked, 'What about you, Paul? Are you working yet?' I shook my head and then stated, 'No, but I am looking. I've wrote after lots of vacancies but as yet, I've had no luck. I'm sure I will eventually, though.' Tom took a sip from his pint and then asked, 'Well, would you be interested in working a few hours a week for the supporters' club?' I smiled before probing further by asking, 'I might be. What does it involve?'

Tom paused for a few seconds and then revealed, 'Sending out souvenirs, arranging away trips – that kind of thing. It's only voluntary but it'll give you valuable work experience, which would probably help you to get a job in the future because you add it to your CV. Plus I'd give you a really good reference, which would also be beneficial when you apply for similar paid roles.' I nodded in Tom's direction and said, 'Yes, you are right, it would certainly help me with my future job search, I have no doubts about that. I'm definitely interested. But can I think about it and let you know tomorrow?' Tom smiled and replied, 'No problem. Give me a ring if you fancy doing it.' He then turned his head and spotted some people at the bar and waved in their direction. Tom then wrote his telephone number on a beer mat which was already on the table and left it with me before saying, 'Don't forget to call me, as I really think we could help each other out.' I smiled and then stated, 'I won't. And thanks for offering me the opportunity.' Tom nodded, then glanced at Ian and Lynn and said, 'Nice to meet you both.' He then got up from his seat and headed in the direction of his friends, who were still standing at the bar.

After Tom had gone, Ian glanced at me and said, 'The voluntary work could be a really good opportunity for you, Paul. Like Tom said, it'll be good work experience for you as well.' I nodded and commented, 'I agree. I'll ring him tomorrow, as I didn't want to appear too keen.' Ian nodded before saying, 'That is exactly what I thought you were doing, matey.'

Later that evening, Ian pushed me into my parents' living room. As per usual, my father ignored us as he sat in his chair drinking a glass of beer, pretending to watch the television. However, my mother, who was sitting on the sofa, smiled, then said, 'Hello you two. Do you fancy a cuppa, Ian?' Ian shook his head and replied, 'Not for me Mrs H, I'm off home for my supper. My mam will have it ready by the time I get home.' He then glanced at me and continued, 'See you later Paul.' I smiled and commented, 'No worries buddy, and congratulations on getting that job, I'm really pleased for you.' Ian smiled and replied, 'Thanks Paul.' He then headed towards the passage door.

After Ian had gone, I looked at my parents and asked, 'You'll never guess what?' My mother glanced at me and queried, 'What's that?' With a beaming smile on my face, I revealed, 'Just like Ian, I've been offered a job.' Much to my amusement, my father almost choked on his beer when he heard my revelation. My mother, however, smiled and said, 'That is brilliant, Paul. Well done. What doing?' Not being able to contain my excitement any longer, I blurted out, 'Order clerk at the football club.' Again my mother smiled before asking, 'How much does it pay?' I revealed, 'Just my expenses.' On hearing this, my father smirked gleefully and stated, 'So, it's not a proper job because they're not paying you.' I nodded and explained, 'Yes, but it is work experience, Dad; something that will help me to get a paid job in the long term.' My mother looked at him and said, 'Paul is right and at least he will be doing something worthwhile, Norman. So, leave the lad alone.' He shook his head and slyly stated, 'Bloody cheap labour if you ask me.' This comment really annoyed her and she glared at my father and shouted, 'Well no one did.' He put his head down and that was the end of that particular conversation!

The following day, I rang Tom and informed him that I'd love to take on the role. He sounded really pleased that I'd decided to accept his offer.

In the next chapter, I shall go into detail regarding incidents that occurred during what I have to say was a most enjoyable time at the Darlington FC Supporters' Club.

Chapter 27

LIKE I said at the end of the last chapter, I really enjoyed my time at Darlington FC Supporters' Club and one story in particular springs to mind.

One morning, I pushed myself into Tom's front room where we used to have our weekly catch-up. On my knee I was carrying former Darlington striker David Speedie's home shirt, with the famous number six emblazoned on the back of it.

For those of you who don't know, Darlington had just sold David to Chelsea for £65,000. He went on to have a brilliant career in football and played for Chelsea, Coventry City, Liverpool, Blackburn Rovers and Southampton, as well as several other clubs on loan near the end of his career. He also represented Scotland at senior level; in his time, he was a top, top player. I still speak to him every so often, which is great and one day, when I was in Doncaster a few years back, I met him for a pub lunch and I have to say, it was awesome to talk over old times with him.

Anyway, back to my tale. I held the shirt up towards Tom and beamed, 'Look what I've brought to show you.

My mate Gavin got me this from David Speedie. Gavin surprised me and took me to Darlington Cricket Club where David was waiting to give me the shirt. I was overwhelmed [I had no idea what was happening] that Gavin had done that for me. I'll keep this shirt for ever; of that there's no doubt.' Tom smiled and responded by saying, 'I bet you will. It was a lovely thing for Gavin to do for you.' I nodded and replied, 'It certainly was.' I still have that shirt to this day and it is one of my most treasured possessions and is now worth quite a lot of money to a collector. It goes without saying that I wouldn't dream of ever selling it. Speaking of match-worn shirts, I now have well over 400 different Darlington ones. However, David Speedie one remains my favourite.

Anyway, getting back to my tale (again), and after a few seconds, Tom looked at me and asked, 'How are you getting on with organising the supporters' club event, Paul?' I smirked and then replied, 'Don't worry. It's all sorted, my friend. It's going to be a great night.' Tom nodded before saying, 'I'm sure it will.'

A week later, Tom was on stage at a local hotel when he hosted the event I'd organised. A strippers night!

I made sure that I was sat at the back of the room (the players, including club captain Kevan Smith and midfielder Roger Wicks, who lived in my street at that particular time, and I shall talk about him in a bit more detail later, were sat in the front row), out of the way as Tom addressed the audience and said, 'Now, then, gentlemen, bit of order please. Can I have one of you players up here on the stage.' Wolf whistles and cheers could then be heard as one of the players, who shall remain unnamed, egged on by his team-mates, was bundled on to the stage. The audience then began to chant, 'Johnny! Johnny! Johnny!'

Tom then nodded to someone in the wings as the music began. As if by magic, two female strippers emerged from backstage. They then went across and sat the by-now very nervous player down on a chair. Rather amusingly to me and indeed the audience, they then proceeded to remove his shirt and massage his chest with baby oil. I was laughing my head off by this time. Tom then came back on stage, smirked and then announced, 'Gentlemen, I think our centre-forward has once again scored tonight!'

It was a brilliant night. However, as I sat there laughing, little did I know what the after-effects would be, for both me and indeed the players who were at the event.

Before I enlighten the reader on what happened following the 'Gentlemen's Evening', I'd like to say a few words about Roger Wicks, whom I've known since 1980.

Roger married a girl called Valerie who lived in my street and that's how I first met him; I was still at school then.

Eventually he and Valerie got their own place but we kept in touch and over the years he, like many other former players, has supported me in whatever I have done. For example, he has played in many charity football matches that I've organised and he even put some money into our film – as did dozens of other former players, and I have to say that I'm extremely grateful to each and every one of them – *Give Them Wings*, which came out to much acclaim in July 2022. I'm pleased to say that Roger and I are still in regular contact to this day and I regard him as a friend, and one day I hope to collaborate with him on a script, as he is now a writer.

Sorry, I got sidetracked yet again, so it is about time that I returned to my story.

The following day, I was summoned to manager Billy Elliott's office to explain what had gone on the previous evening.

A stern-faced Billy was sitting behind a large desk with me directly opposite him. It was like being back at school. I tried not to smile as I thought of the time Malcolm and I tried to run away and I ended up in the headmaster's office with my mother. I was brought back from my trance when I noticed Kevan Smith gleefully watching the proceedings from a rear window, invisible to the manager.

After a few seconds, Billy looked at me and asked, 'So, Paul, tell me, how old are you?' I hesitated, not quite sure whether to admit that I was actually under age, but thought it best to be honest so I responded by replying, 'I'm 17, boss.' Billy shook his head in disbelief and stated in a raised voice, 'Seventeen! So you're not even old enough to drink, never mind organise this fiasco.' I put my head down before saying quietly, 'No, Billy.' At this stage of my telling-off, I was doing my utmost to avoid eye contact with Kevan, who was now trying to get a reaction by grinning at me through the window. Billy attracted my attention by stating, again in a raised voice, 'Given your age, I can't believe you were responsible for hiring those bloody strippers.' I half-smiled and said, 'I just thought it would be a bit of fun, boss.' Billy shook his head angrily and then in an even more raised voice stated, 'Fun! You reckon? Well I can tell you it certainly wasn't fun to have my bloody ear chewed off all day by the press.' Once again, I was distracted by Kevan, who was still grinning at me. Unfortunately, on this occasion, I was no longer unable to contain myself and burst out laughing. Quite rightly, Billy was incensed and shouted, 'It's not funny, boy!' I tried my best to control myself and shook my head and responded by saying, 'No, Billy. I'm really sorry.' Billy paused for a few seconds and passed his 'sentence' by stating, 'Right. You're banned from the ground for one week and that includes matches. Get out of my sight and send Kevan in before I really lose my temper.'

Looking back, despite him telling me off – rightly so in my opinion – I really liked Billy. On a couple of occasions, he gave whoever I was with and I a lift back to Darlington on the team bus. One such time was Wimbledon away in season 1982/83 after our train was cancelled. As well as that, he was always very kind to me and I was sad when he was sacked in May 1983. Many years later, I was sorry to hear that he'd passed away at the age of 82. One final comment about him: he never did find out that Kevan was grinning at me and that was why I ended up bursting out laughing. I'm still in touch with Kevan to this day, and I still giggle when we mention that incident, even after all the years that have gone by.

In the six years I volunteered for the supporters' club, I met some brilliant people. These include Kevan Smith, David Speedie, Alan Walsh, Roger Wicks, David Young, Mark Forster, the late, great Cyril Knowles, Bob Paisley (at a dinner), Lawrie McMenemy (at a fundraising match in 1982), Brian Clough (when Darlington's reserves played Nottingham Forest), and many, many others. As well as Roger and Kevan, I'm still in touch with Alan Walsh, Paul Ward, Dale Anderson, Gary Hyde, David Speedie, David Young and Mark Forster, who all played for the club during this period, to this day, which is good. I'm also in touch with many others whom I met after moving on from the supporters' club. These include former manager David Hodgson, Neil Wainwright, Louis Laing, Simon Shaw, Gary Twynham, Peter Kirkham, Gary Brown, Mark Barnard, Joey Hope and Jack Winstanley.

A final comment on one player who has become a good friend from that er, Mark Forster – he promised to throw me his shirt after the promotion-clinching game at Crewe Alexandra in season 1984/85. Anyway, I caught it, but some moron wrenched it out of my hand and within a few seconds, it was gone for ever. I can remember being gutted at the time. Strangely enough, some 14 years later, I bumped into Mark at a Darlington FC reunion. In the course of our conversation, I happened to mention this incident. When he heard my tale, he promised to give me a signed shirt from the promotion-winning season. True to his word, he posted it through my letterbox the following day. From that day on, we became firm friends, and have remained so ever since. Mark attended my wedding and also wrote the foreword for my book *Give Them Wings*, which was published in April 2021, for which I was eternally grateful.

Anyway, returning to the matter in hand, and despite loving my role with the supporters' club, in 1987, I decided that I needed to do more with my life and keep the promise I made to my mother to go to college. So that is exactly what I did.

I shall talk about this in the next chapter.

Chapter 28

AS I mentioned in the previous chapter, in 1987 I decided to do something different with my life and return to education. I loved my voluntary job with Darlington FC Supporters' Club, but I felt the time was right for a change of direction. I therefore made an appointment at my local Job Centre with a DRO (disability resettlement officer, as they were called at that time) and he advised me that in order to improve my prospects of finding work, I should consider going for a six-week assessment at Preston Rehabilitation Centre to find out what my strengths and weaknesses were. He explained that the centre catered specifically for the training and employment needs of disabled people. My mother was naturally over the moon when I told her what the DRO had suggested in the interview. I knew it meant a hell of a lot to her that I'd finally kept the promise I'd made to her when I left school. I had always intended to keep it and I just knew in my own mind that this was now the right time to do it.

However, rather than supporting me, as per usual, my father said I was wasting my time because no one would consider employing anyone in a wheelchair. Not for the first time in my life, I was determined to prove him wrong. Incidentally, by this time, my father was 'retired'. He had been on the sick for months on end (I don't think that he had any intention of returning to work) and one day a representative from his place of work (I use that word very loosely in his case because from what he told me, he did very little while he was there) basically told him that due to his very poor sickness record, they had decided to pay him off. He was actually over the moon about it. I have to say, if that had been me, I would have been embarrassed. Here I was desperate to forge a working career, and he threw his down the drain, simply because of his idleness. It really annoyed me that he simply didn't care. Once he was as good as sacked, he made no attempt whatsoever to find work, while my mother worked her fingers to the bone by having two jobs to keep the house going. I never forgave him for that; more importantly, neither did my mother.

Anyway, back to my story. My six-week course at Preston Rehabilitation Centre, August and September 1987, was a revelation. The only drawback as I saw it was the fact that, due to the nature of the place, there was a high turnover of people, so you never really got a chance to know anyone properly. In a sense, it was like a conveyor belt.

However, on the plus side, I tried loads of different jobs and eventually it was decided that an administration role would be most beneficial to me. I agreed with that assessment, given that I volunteered at Darlington Football Club doing mostly administration tasks, so I had the relevant experience.

Sadly, halfway through my course, my friendship with Tom ended on a sour note; something that I have to say, I was really sad about.

You can imagine my surprise and indeed shock when the police paid me a visit at Preston Rehabilitation Centre in connection with discrepancies with the supporters' club bank account.

After a brief interview, which I have to say was embarrassing, simply because it made me look bad to the staff at Preston when I had done absolutely nothing wrong, I agreed to speak to them again when I got home the following weekend.

When I did see them, they asked me about some money which had gone missing from the account. I said that I didn't know anything about it, and when they checked the dates the funds had been withdrawn, they knew that I couldn't have been responsible because I was in Preston at the time, even though my signature had been used, which I found extremely disappointing and indeed annoying to say the very least.

I'd known Tom for six years but, with the benefit of hindsight, he'd always struck me as a bit of a shady character; something that I should have done more about. In my defence, I was very young at the time. However, I can recall one incident in particular when

I was a member of the supporters' club committee. The football club chairman had asked Tom where the money was and he'd replied that it was at my house in a cupboard. I didn't know that he was going to say this prior to the meeting, otherwise I would never have agreed to back him up. The chairman was none too pleased by this explanation and said, 'You mean to tell me that over £1,000 of our money is being kept in a cupboard in Paul's house?' Foolishly, to protect Tom, I went along with his cock and bull story, something that I've regretted ever since. Following the meeting, I made it clear to him that I wouldn't be put in that position again.

Later, I found out that he had borrowed money from my father and not repaid it in full. Apparently, Tom had promised him a big interest percentage in return for lending him the money. With this in mind, I did have a wry smile on my face when he didn't get it all back because he shouldn't have been so greedy in expecting a big return; that was the only reason that my father lent him the money. Later, I also learned that Tom also borrowed money from many other people, some of whom I knew as well, and he didn't pay them back either. Looking back, this wasn't a good thing to say the very least.

These acts of dishonesty led to him being arrested and he was eventually sent for trial. After being found guilty, he lost his business and his house and was jailed for 18 months for deception. This was a sad end for someone who had been a good friend to me for many years.

One final comment regarding Tom: I'd always liked him and would have tried to help him if I could but after he'd signed my name for the bank, I knew without doubt that there was no going back. I was sad about this, but in my heart of hearts, I knew that I was doing the right thing.

There I go again, getting sidetracked. So once again, back to my tale. While I was at Preston I met people who had far greater problems than me, and this really made me think that despite being a wheelchair user, in many ways, I was very lucky. As my mother always said, 'There's always someone worse off than you, Paul.' As per usual, she was right. I'd seen proof of this twice in my life, once at Percy Hedley School and then at Preston Rehabilitation Centre.

Fortunately, every other weekend my mother and father came to collect me by car. After the assessment was over I was advised to go to Finchale Training College in Durham and they put my name down since there was a one-year waiting list, which at the time, I was disappointed about.

However, as luck would have it, that year turned out to be very entertaining and indeed enjoyable.

Chapter 29

IN JANUARY 1989 my mother and I, after many discussions, reached probably the most momentous decision in our lives at that time. We planned to leave my father and move into a council flat. Even now after all this time and despite the fact that my father is no longer with us, I know that we made the correct decision. He brought it all on himself over many years as his behaviour was really difficult to live with on a daily basis. He wouldn't work when he was perfectly capable of doing so which resulted in my mother having two jobs while he was either racing his pigeons or fast asleep in his chair. He could and indeed should have done a hell of a lot more to make my mother's life easier (getting a job and indeed not pulling sickies for three or four months at a time would have certainly been a start), but that he chose not to was his choice, not mine nor my mother's. With this in mind, he had no one to blame but himself. In addition, he didn't treat me very well to say the least, which is another reason that I didn't have any sympathy for him and I still don't to this day.

You might think I'm being cold-hearted now that he's no longer here. Maybe I am, but if someone treats you badly for long enough and constantly puts you down day after day, which he did, then you end up having no respect for that person and that was certainly the case with me. With this in mind, I certainly don't feel guilty for feeling that way.

Anyway, we ended up making all the arrangements regarding the move without him knowing, which actually was quite a feat. Ironically, he was actually celebrating his 55th birthday at Hopetown and Whessoe Working Men's Club on the evening we headed off into the sunset to start our new lives. We simply hired a removal van, which a friend drove, took a few items of furniture and left him to his own devices. I for one didn't feel guilty at all and was glad to be away from him. I know that my mother felt exactly the same way.

One final comment on this situation that I feel I must make. Later, my father accused me of splitting his marriage up, which certainly wasn't the case. He made a damn good job of that himself and certainly didn't need my help to do it. It was me who acquired the flat from the council, and yes I did ask my mother whether she wanted to come with me. However, I said that if she didn't want to, I would understand and that I would employ carers to look after me. My mother insisted that this was the opportunity she'd waited for and that she wanted to accompany me on the next chapter of my life. I did say that it had to be her choice; she assured me that it was. So despite what my father said, I wasn't a marriage-wrecker.

Although my mother left my father a note to say that we were leaving, it goes without saying that we didn't leave him a forwarding address. However, he still managed to find out where we were living within a couple of weeks of us leaving him. He came to the flat and very sheepishly took me to one side in my bedroom and literally begged me to go back to Dundee Street with him because he was lonely and was struggling to cope on his own. I steadfastly refused and so he departed, without speaking one word to my mother.

The ground-floor flat was in an awful mess when we first moved in. I was appalled when we saw it for the first time. When my mother decorated the place, she uncovered 16 layers of wallpaper before she eventually reached bare plaster!

The council installed a floor shower in the bathroom; outside the flat they erected a handrail and laid some concrete paving slabs to make a ramp for my wheelchair.

This was certainly a hectic period for me because we moved on a Friday and I started my business studies course the following Monday at Finchale Training College. Since I could hardly ask my father to take me to the college in his car, my mother took me to the train station on my first day and when I arrived in Durham a minibus from the college was waiting to collect me and take me on to my final destination.

Chapter 30

MY FIRST impressions of Finchale Training College and its surroundings were distinctly favourable. The building was set in its own tree-lined grounds, which were very pleasant indeed. Moreover, the college, like Percy Hedley School, catered solely for students with disabilities.

Within the college there were three main departments: one that taught clock and watch repair; another that offered instruction in horticulture; and last, but by no means least, business studies. It was in the latter department that I undertook a course in secretarial studies as given the experience I'd gained with Darlington Supporters' Club, together with the advice I had received from the staff at Preston Rehabilitation Centre, this was the correct choice for me.

Having already sampled residential life at Percy Hedley and Preston Rehabilitation Centre, I soon settled in. The facilities at the college were quite adequate, though very outdated. The room, which I shared with another wheelchair user called Mark, had two single beds, two wardrobes and a sink. If we needed a hot drink there was a coffee vending machine situated in one of the corridors, which we used quite a bit.

Also on site, there was a laundry. However, after thinking about it, I opted to take my dirty washing home at the weekend as this was both easier and indeed cheaper for me.

Unfortunately, in my opinion, the college food was of a poor standard. Although there was always a wide selection on the menu, mainly due to overcooking, in my opinion it was good food spoiled. This was a shame because, if a little more care from the chefs had been taken, the end results would certainly have been much better. I once said that to one of them. It didn't go down very well. A bit like some of their food!

In addition to the facilities already mentioned, there was also a refectory and a bar that opened between 6.30pm and 11pm, but I went out most nights into Durham, so I didn't make use of them very often as I found the college to be rather strict when it came to students having to return to their rooms at what I considered to be an unreasonable hour.

As a case in point, I could give you the following example. On a Wednesday evening a video was shown on the television in the communal lounge. But what annoyed me was that the college staff tended to be rather inflexible when it came to turning it off at 11 o'clock sharp. This meant that in practice people who were watching the video, which didn't finish until a few minutes after the deadline, would miss the end of the film, as a member of the night staff would come in, walk up to the VCR machine, and remove the tape. Obviously the students didn't like this happening, but unfortunately there was nothing they could do about it. It was like being back at Percy Hedley School!

Despite these minor gripes, overall I did quite like it there and things got even better for me personally when I struck up a really good friendship with a lad called David Parker, who was from Northallerton. David was studying an accountancy course and would give me regular lifts back home on a Friday afternoon and pick me up for the return journey on a Sunday. As time went by, with his help, I managed to take more and more of my belongings with me to Durham, including a kettle and a portable black and white television. Having these things in my room certainly made my life much better and indeed more comfortable.

During this period my mother worked part-time in the evening as an office cleaner for a firm of solicitors based in Darlington. Essentially, we were both very happy doing our own thing. At weekends I went to the football with Ian and some other friends (mainly John Gray, whom I first met in 1981 and we are still great friends to this day) while my mother had her own circle of friends with whom she loved to go to the bingo. It therefore worked out extremely well for us both. We were much happier than we had been when we lived with my father.

Another thing that I loved about my mother was if I wanted to go to a nightclub it was never a problem with her. Basically, she never stopped me from doing anything that I wanted to do. I'll always be grateful to her for that. In other words, she treated me like any normal, able-bodied 23-year-old son. In fairness, she had never treated me any different because of my disability so thinking about it I shouldn't have expected anything less.

Returning to my story: college life was certainly eventful and exciting. I can remember that on my 24th birthday in March 1989, my classmates booked me a strippergram. The girl took most of my clothes off, which shocked me quite a bit, but then she took most of hers off as well, so that made it all worthwhile! After that we went out on the town into Durham and went on a massive pub crawl. How the hell I got up the following morning I'll never know. I certainly had a hangover, that's for sure! But it was a good night, one that I didn't forget for a long time.

So, there I was, trying to keep up with my studies during the daytime and going out on the drink most nights with my classmates.

Fortunately for me, my typing tutor, Maureen Summers, was very perceptive and worked out what was happening. One day she took me to one side and said, 'Paul, if you don't slow down a bit and sort yourself out you are going to blow everything.'

Maureen's comment certainly made me think. And it was the way she said it. She didn't tell me to stop going out, she just pointed out that my grades were going down and advised me to reconsider my priorities. That really made me wake up to my responsibilities.

Although I didn't stop going out completely, I did so much less, and I have to say that I put a hell of a lot more effort into my studies. This had an impact as my grades, went up instantly, almost as if by magic.

One final comment on Maureen Summers: to this day, I'm convinced that if it hadn't been for her noticing and politely telling me where I was going wrong, I know 100 per cent that I would never have passed the course and got a job later on. I've therefore got a lot to thank her for.

Those college days were certainly some of the best ones of my life on a social level. A group of us used to catch a bus to Durham from the college every Thursday night (the only night I went out after my chat with Maureen) and would go on a pub crawl. To this day, I can recall that our favourite pubs in the city were the Market Tavern, the Hogshead, the Fighting Cocks and the Angel, which was up a huge hill.

We were a group of like-minded disabled people, who each had their own problems one way or other, and yet we all got on really well as a group. There was Jason from Bradford, who as with Colin, who was also part of the group, had lost a leg in a car accident; Ian from Newcastle, who had a back injury; and a guy called Richard, who hailed from the south coast. Looking back, some of the things we got up to during that time don't bear thinking about now!

Returning to college life, I can vividly remember on one occasion I'd accidentally left my plastic bottle I use for urinating behind in my room.

Being a wheelchair user means that I can't stand up at a urinal, so instead I use a plastic bottle and then I empty it down the toilet, before washing it out. Since I needed to go rather urgently, instead of making for the toilet down the corridor, in order to save time (I was due back in class in ten minutes) I decided to do it in my room and empty the bottle down the sink. It goes without saying that I rinsed both the bottle and indeed the sink out.

Colin was with me at the time and saw a middle-aged female cleaner walking past my bedroom door, which was slightly ajar. Smirking, he shouted: 'Hey, missus, come and have a look at this!' The cleaner walked in and saw me with the bottle in my hand and my trousers round my ankles. When she saw what I was doing she exclaimed, 'That is absolutely disgusting,' and promptly burst into tears, which I thought was a complete overreaction, given that she didn't see anything because my private parts were covered by the urine bottle.

It came as no surprise to me when she reported us both to Maureen Summers who, to our great relief, laughed the incident off as an innocent prank. She actually found it funny once I explained that the cleaner hadn't seen anything. The cleaner, however, never forgot what had happened and from that moment onwards ignored us and never spoke a word to either Colin or me again, which thinking about it now, was very childish, especially as she was in her 50s. I have to confess, every time I passed her in the corridor I couldn't help smirking just a little bit!

Another funny incident happened one night when Colin and I returned to the college at half past 12 after a session on the booze. Unfortunately, a security guard intercepted us and proceeded to rebuke me about being late – not for the first time, I have to admit.

However, as he was leaning over me and pointing out the error of my ways, I was highly amused to see Colin slowly unzipping his flies and taking out his penis. Unbeknown to the security guard, Colin pretended to slap him over the head with it, but fortunately for us two, the man didn't even notice! It was funny and reminded me of the time when Billy Elliott was telling me off and Kevan Smith was smirking through the window. The only difference was that on this occasion, I managed to control myself and didn't laugh!

Also, after yet another boozy Thursday night out in Durham, the following morning I was running late and to my surprise, Colin was sitting in the hallway having a coffee when I made my entrance.

Normally he'd have been in lessons by then so I asked him what he was doing there. 'I've just got up,' was his innocent reply. Then he continued, 'I can't be bothered going to lessons today. Shall we just get our stuff and go home?' I smirked and then nodded, went to fetch my holdall and we left, without saying a word to anyone. I was back at home just after ten in the morning.

My mother, who was naturally quite surprised to see me, looked me in the eye and asked, 'Paul, are you skiving?' I couldn't lie to her, and admitted that I was, to which she said matter-of-factly, 'That's all I wanted to know. At least you are being honest about it,' and left it at that. I explained that nothing much happened on a Friday morning, so we decided to come home a couple of hours early.

At around that time, I can remember one of our tutors saying that we were the most disruptive group of students he'd ever had. In fact, looking back now, I think the lecturers wrote Fridays off because they were just a waste of time as most of the students were either hung over or in 'go-home mode'.

I have to say that I was lucky to fall in with such a fantastic group of people, because it could quite easily have been the other way around. I could have been stuck with a lot of boring students instead. And yet we all managed to pass our exams. To use the well-worn cliche, we played hard but we worked hard. And that is important, because you always have to remember why you're at college, as Maureen Summers reminded me several times during my stay at Finchale.

When I'd almost completed my course, I wrote to quite a few companies in Darlington asking for a work placement. The first one I obtained was at Cummins Engine Company in Darlington (now sadly closed down). I was put under the wing of a lady called Win Crow and she taught me a lot about work practices. I enjoyed my five weeks there from October to November 1989 in their excellent computer department. Cummins even paid me a wage of £30 a week – this was the maximum I could earn before income tax would have been deducted.

My second work placement followed immediately afterwards at the Employment Service in Darlington. I hated it there and was glad to leave. The majority of the staff seemed to be frightened of me and hardly spoke at all, although a couple of them were pleasant enough.

One final comment regarding college: although my grades had slipped slightly, after I bucked up my ideas I came out with eight qualifications in total. And for the Pitman English for Business Communications I received a first-class pass with a mark of 90 per cent, the only student in my year to achieve such a result. So that wasn't too bad. But I also came away from the place with an awful lot of memories and looking back, these are just as important to me.

So, I left Finchale Training College in 1990 with a fistful of qualifications. But what did I do next? That was the question.

All will be revealed in the epilogue, which follows.

Epilogue

IN MAY of 1990 I sent off a speculative letter to a local agricultural merchant called Farmway Ltd, who were based in Darlington at that particular time. Following an interview, they promised to keep me in mind for any vacancies that might crop up in the future. To be honest, I didn't expect to hear from them again and therefore, I didn't give it another thought.

The following month, much to my surprise, they got in touch with Peter Ray, a gentleman who ran the Sheltered Placement Scheme at that time – a scheme that used government money to pay a percentage of the wages of a disabled person. I had previously spoken to Peter regarding using the scheme and had mentioned it at my original interview at Farmway. The personnel manager remembered me, as the company were actively seeking to employ a disabled person, which was brilliant for me, so I was offered a job as full-time Farmwatch co-ordinator and I was to start in September 1990.

However, although they did everything right when they appointed me, I don't think they gave sufficient thought to what the post would actually entail.

To be absolutely truthful, Farmwatch (liaising with the local farming community and the police to try and prevent crime on farmland) was only really a part-time job, so I was bored with nothing to do a lot of the time. There I was, fresh from a business studies course, with 12 qualifications in total under my belt, typing up internal envelopes! That was hardly a sensible state of affairs. I actually felt brain dead at the end of most days!

However, this turned out to be the last thing on my mind, as my world was turned upside down in 1992 when my mother suffered a major stroke.

I arrived home with a work colleague to find her on the floor, hardly breathing. She was taken to hospital and remained there for a month.

During that time, a friend called Neil Parkinson looked after me until I managed to get carers in place. I was eternally grateful for his help at that time.

When my mother came home, she wasn't the same and with very little support from my family, I struggled to look after her. She was up during the night which was extremely difficult for me at the time.

In 1994, my mother went back to live with my father after trying to set her bed on fire. By this time she had really bad dementia and the fire incident was the last straw. I simply couldn't look after her safely any more.

Unfortunately, she died a week later and I was consumed with guilt and ended up having a breakdown and trying to take my own life.

Luckily, I survived, but to this day, I still feel guilty about letting my mother go back to live with my father. It goes without saying that had I known she'd only had a week left to live, I would never have done so, and it took me many, many years to come to terms with that. Although the guilt remains, I have come to accept that I did it for the right reasons, which certainly helps.

On my return to Farmway after compassionate leave, an opportunity arose when a new personnel manager was employed and I became responsible for the distribution of internal and external vacancies and placing advertisements in the local and national press. I also booked spaces for the company at various agricultural shows throughout the north-east, raised cheques for payment and edited the monthly *Farmway Focus* newsletter. Luckily for me, unlike his predecessor, he saw past my wheelchair and soon realised that I was more than capable of doing these tasks and therefore ensured that I got a decent computer to use, rather than an ancient electric typewriter which I'd been expected to use previously. I actually enjoyed my work during that time as I felt fulfilled.

However, nothing lasts for ever and in 1996 I was transferred to Farmway Boilercare, a company that serviced and indeed installed both oil and gas boilers.

I was responsible for planning the engineers' routes. I enjoyed it to an extent, but I felt like I wasn't really wanted there, especially after the original manager retired. So in 1998 I applied for, and indeed got, a job as a claims administrator at County Durham Training and Enterprise Council (TEC).

Coincidentally, when I took up my post, I found myself working in the very same building in Valley Street, Darlington, where I'd spent my work placement with the Employment Service back in 1989.

I didn't really like this job because it was too labour intensive for me (I also seemed to be playing 'catch-up') and on some occasions, due to my disability, I struggled to keep up with the tight deadlines for work to be completed. I should explain that this was not due to a lack of knowledge, as I knew the claims process inside out. Anyway, after a lot of soul searching, I applied for an internal transfer in 1999.

With all of the above in mind, when the opportunity arose to join the Lifelong Learning Team I jumped at the chance.

My new job involved working on a database that collated information relating to individual learning accounts (ILAs).

In a nutshell, people could apply for money for training from the TECs and my job was to ensure that each request for assistance was properly processed. I have to admit that it was a job I really enjoyed doing and more importantly to me, it was a lot less labour-intensive.

Unfortunately, for the second time in my working career, things changed. Let me explain.

In early 2000 I changed jobs – my ILA administrator role was deemed redundant and was passed on to a different company called Capita.

I was offered the chance of a job there and actually went for a visit but wasn't at all impressed by what I witnessed.

Every time I left my desk I would have to sign out, and the idea of giving them the contract in my opinion was a recipe for disaster as in my opinion they clearly didn't have even a basic understanding of ILAs.

My fears were confirmed later when they actually lost the contract, and needless to say, I turned down their offer of a job.

In between times I also applied to what was then called the Employment Service (now the Department of Work and Pensions) and was lucky enough to obtain a job as a contracts administrator, which was to be based at Birtley near Chester-le-Street. Aubrey Form, my former manager at County Durham TEC, and a man I respected very much and still do to this day, also started on the same day as I did. I was glad about this as at least he was someone I knew.

The job involved dealing with training providers who were contracted to run the New Deal scheme.

The colleagues I had at Birtley Job Centre were the best that I have ever worked with. Julia, who was the manager, is a person who I have come to respect over the years. She was hard but fair. Then there was Pat McMahon, who later wrote a song entitled 'Man of Steel' which was used in our film *Give Them Wings*. Pat was a singer with a local band and I therefore went to see them play on a few occasions. The drummer was quite famous as he had been in the Toy Dolls, whose claim to fame was a number one hit called 'Nellie the Elephant'.

The remainder of the people in our team were great and I got on well with every single one of them, which was brilliant.

As I've mentioned before, nothing lasts for ever and unfortunately, due to a reorganisation within the now renamed DWP in 2003, Birtley Job Centre was closed and this heralded the start of a process of me moving offices three times in 18 months. I was really disappointed, because I loved my job and got on really well with my colleagues.

This is what happened during this sometimes very unsettling period.

The people I worked with at Birtley were relocated to an inaccessible office in Gateshead, which meant I had to work at South Shields.

I was still part of the team and I kept in touch with the rest of them by phone; while it had not been an ideal situation, I made the best of it and simply got on with my job.

The staff at South Shields were really pleasant and made me welcome. I sometimes helped them out by inputting forms on to a database when I wasn't doing my own job.

I was happy there until my next move in July 2005 which was to Durham Job Centre Plus.

I have to say that this was a total culture shock for me after the relaxed atmosphere I'd experienced with the Gateshead team.

My team leader and indeed the team manager were really strict, something that I hadn't been used to at all. At Gateshead I'd been allowed just to get on with my job as the rest of the guys in our team had faith in me.

At Durham things were done differently, and sometimes in my opinion not as efficiently as I'd been used to and I found this extremely frustrating.

However, things changed after yet another reorganisation (I was getting used to them by then) and the manager was replaced by Julia, with whom I'd got on very well at Birtley.

It was at this time that everyone had to apply for their own jobs. After the interview I knew I hadn't been successful. (I found it disappointing that someone I'd known for only a few months interviewed me as she didn't have the time to see what I was capable of.) This proved to be the case some months later when the results of the interviews came out and the person who'd been there the longest and was a friend of the supervisor got the job. Although I felt hard done by, I accepted the decision, rather than bothering to appeal.

This meant that I was placed on the surplus list. I continued to work at Durham, and in the meantime I started applying for other jobs within the DWP. I went for one job at Sunderland but the manager there didn't think the job would be any good for me. While being disappointed once more, I did think that she had a point.

One afternoon I was looking at the job vacancies on the intranet and spotted one for the Pension Service. I applied for it and received a letter stating I'd got an interview.

Following that interview, I was successful in getting the position and started working there in June 2006.

Starting there the same day were Chris Walkers from Durham and Ian Robinson from Whitley Bay. We got chatting in training and I have stayed friends with Chris to this day.

Following my training, I was placed in a Pension Credit Change of Circumstances team. Just by way of an explanation, in simple terms, pension credit is income support for pensioners.

My role was to process the changes pensioners reported to us to ensure they receive the correct amount of benefit. I really enjoyed the work; I also met some really fantastic people.

In 2008, after yet another re-organisation, I was moved to the mortgage section. This was a good move for me as the role I was given involved me handling less paperwork which suited me fine.

I stayed with the Pension Service until 2018 when due to the after-effects of a serious car accident I was forced to retire.

On the whole I enjoyed my time there, though I have to admit that following my return to work after the car crash, things weren't easy. Thinking about it now, I went back too soon and I struggled physically. I could do my job well enough, but in a nutshell, my body failed me as it wasn't, and indeed still isn't, strong enough for the rigours of full-time employment.

One final comment: I feel that I could have been supported more following my car crash (as I mentioned in *Give Them Wings*), but that's water under the bridge now and I've moved on with my life.

It is now time to tell you about the car crash that has changed my life so much. So here goes.

I'd arranged to meet my friend and former Darlington striker Dale Anderson at a pub called the Gretna in Newton Aycliffe, which for those of you who don't know, is just outside Darlington.

Jayne, my then PA, accompanied me. The pair of us made the journey in a taxi.

The driver seemed to be in a rush and had already cleared my job (he'd lied and said to the controller that he'd already dropped me off) so was under pressure to get me to my destination as his next fare was expecting him, plus he was getting stick from the controller on the radio.

Anyway, when we got to the pub entrance, he missed the turning, so he had to go to the end of the dual carriageway and turn around and come back up on the south side, rather than the north.

To my amazement, he missed the turning again, so had to go to the other end of the road to turn around.

On his third and final attempt, the idiot again missed the turning, but on this occasion he lost his temper and proceeded to perform a u-turn, and was hit by an oncoming car at 60mph.

The next thing I remember for certain is being cut out of the taxi by firemen and being rushed to James Cook Hospital.

Jayne, who wasn't hurt as badly as me, contacted Ian, who rushed to the crash site and waited for me to be cut out of the taxi, then accompanied me to the hospital, where I stayed for three days, before signing myself out, as the personal care I was getting wasn't the best simply because they didn't have the staff to look after a severely disabled person like me.

During my stay in hospital, it transpired that I'd suffered three broken ribs, a back injury, head and facial injuries plus severe bruising to my body.

On my return home I employed a temporary PA called Peter who looked after me alongside Ian at home.

Jayne did return to work, but looking back, I don't think she recovered mentally from the accident and left my employment within a few months.

Peter, on the other hand, was taken on permanently and another PA was also taken on making a total of three staff employed by me, including Ian.

My recovery was long and slow and after almost five years, I received some compensation for my injuries and trauma. However, I'd far rather have my health back to what it was pre-crash, without a doubt, but as I've learned, life isn't always fair and I just accepted my lot and got on with things.

Changing the subject rather rapidly, over my lifetime, like any man, I've had a few relationships here and there. However, I didn't meet the love of my life until I was in my 50s. Let me enlighten you.

In early 2016, I got chatting to a lady called Jennifer on Facebook. Little did I know for certain (though I always thought it could happen) that I'd end up falling in love with this brilliant lady and that she would change my life for the better.

Before long, we were seeing each other every day, and in 2017, we got married.

I can honestly say that despite us both being ill with the flu, it was still the best day of my life, one that I'll never forget. The wedding itself was absolutely fantastic. Ian, Mark Forster, John Gray and many other friends were there.

Another huge plus for me is that I was accepted into Jen's family, which was great. Jeana, Jemma and Jennifer (Jen's children) became my family, and remain so to this day.

The brilliant thing is Jen and I are as happy now as we were on our wedding day and I can honestly say that she truly is the love of my life.

The next thing to mention is the 20-year journey Ian and I had to get *Give Them Wings* over the line.

In October 2000 Ben (not his real name) and I, in the company of several other Darlington fans, one of whom was visually impaired, made the journey to Hartlepool by train for the derby match against our local rivals.

While waiting for the connecting service at Thornaby train station, the lads were engaged in some typical pre-match banter, which was basically taking the mickey out of each other and being very loud in the process.

Unbeknown to us, while this was taking place, a guy was filming us on a camcorder.

He later introduced himself as Nick Rowntree and explained that at the time he was a media studies student at Teesside University and said that the banter between me and the lads was so funny that he couldn't resist filming it. He added that he was an actor from Norton and was now a screenwriter on the lookout for a suitable project. I then mentioned that I had recently had a book published and that he would be more than welcome to have a look to see if he liked the story, with the intention of making either a short film or a documentary based on it. Nick seemed quite interested in my suggestion and gave me his business card and asked me to either email or ring him.

The following Monday I rang Nick and he agreed to call at my house to pick up a copy of *Flipper's Side* in order that he could assess it to see if it could be made into a film script. As promised he turned up and collected the book and said he'd be in touch later. To be honest, I never expected to hear from him again.

However, how wrong I was! Within a couple of weeks Nick came back and said that he had now set up a company called Plot 73 and also that he wanted to buy the rights to the book. Ben and I were amazed. Since my autobiography had only been on sale for three months now either a feature film or a documentary could be made about it. Even though we had both realised that our work had the potential for such a development we never dreamed things would move so rapidly.

Nick said he'd get a contract drawn up giving him rights to the film for a mutually agreed period.

During the following months Nick worked on the script – he seemed genuinely determined to get the project off the ground.

The following year he persuaded local director Scott Mann to become involved with the project and changed the name of the company from Plot 73 to Shakabuku Films.

Funding was awarded through Northern Film & Media for the script development, which helped Nick a great deal.

After completing the first draft, Nick and Scott took it to the Cannes Film Festival in May 2002, thanks to Northern Film & Media, but we all knew that it was going to be a long haul before the film would eventually be made.

Unfortunately, despite working on the project for five years, and also going through several versions of the script, Scott and Nick appeared no nearer to getting my autobiography on to the big screen. Ben and I therefore spoke at great length about this and thought it might be time to go down a different avenue as Shakabuku Films had since taken on another project called *The Tournament*, relegating our film, now called *Down Amongst the Dead Men*, to the back burner.

In 2005, Ben, Ian and I met a guy called Andy Isaac at a meeting at Darlington Football Club (actor Bill Fellows was also there). Andy was a film producer and seemed well equipped to take our project to the next stage. How wrong we were.

Once our contract with Shakabuku Films had expired in September 2006, the four of us set up our own company, Down Amongst the Dead Men Productions Ltd, with the aim of getting the film made. I have to say, it was great to have Ian on board.

Despite Andy writing several scripts over a two-year period, none of which were good enough, our relationship with him began to deteriorate as once again we weren't getting anywhere fast.

Eventually, we decided to go our separate ways; this heralded the start of what could only be described as a nightmare and at the time could have resulted in us losing the rights to our own film!

It all started when Ian and I went on the train to meet Andy (by this time Ben had resigned from the company) to try and sort things out regarding his 'script', which during our journey to London, we had made more than 100 changes to.

When we presented Andy with our suggested improvements he haughtily dismissed the work that we'd done as 'wank'. Not being prepared to discuss our changes in a constructive manner showed us the true nature of the man. This was someone who couldn't accept criticism. This meeting spelled the end of our association with Andy and consequently when Cannes came around again in May we decided not to attend.

However, to our annoyance, Andy rang me to say that he was still pursuing the project. Things became even more awkward when I learned that he had sent the screenplay to various actors such as Emma Thompson. Goodness knows what they must have thought when presented with Andy's dire literary efforts.

In June, Ian and I resigned as directors of the company and in October of the same year we made the first application to have the company struck off. But despite having asked Andy to abandon the project he insisted on pursuing it.

After speaking to Ben, we decided to seek legal assistance to prevent Andy from exploiting a story to which he did not own the copyright.

We therefore took out an injunction against him which we hoped would stop him in his tracks. Andy, for his part, insisted that he was free to pursue the project as the screenplay was his own invention and therefore did not represent a breach of copyright. We were now headed on a collision course.

As you can imagine, we also had money to find for legal expenses as well as several hundred pounds to pay for an after-the-event insurance that would compensate us if we actually lost the case. Andy, however, took no legal advice and throughout the whole affair represented himself. After two appearances in court at Newcastle-upon-Tyne we agreed to mediation with Andy, hoping that we could resolve the matter without incurring ever more costs.

During the mediation at our solicitor's offices in Thornaby, Andy agreed to rewrite the screenplay in such a way that he would remove any links to my story. Ben and I were happy to agree to this and we subsequently waited to see the revised script which should have ended the matter once and for all.

Unfortunately, when the promised script arrived, it soon became clear that no substantial changes had been made. Even my mother's name remained unchanged and key incidents from *Flipper's Side* remained unaltered.

By this time, with the legal fees mounting, we had no alternative but to take Andy to the Patents Court in London. This would now be the final stage of the process and a judge would decide whether we were in the right or not.

Ben, Ian and I travelled down to London with an air of expectation. Our solicitor, Alex Smith, was confident that we would win, which helped settle our nerves.

The proceedings turned out to be very interesting indeed. Once again Andy represented himself, which meant that the judge had to allow him a certain amount of leeway given the fact that he was up against a trained barrister.

Nevertheless, there was a limit to Judge Birss's patience. On one occasion, after Andy had given one of his characteristic rambling replies, he asked the judge if that was OK. 'No, that is not OK, Mr Isaac,' came the withering reply.

When I was in the witness box and Andy was questioning me, I tried to be as calm as possible and not lose my temper. Ben, however, struggled to contain the obvious dislike which he felt for Andy and became annoyed by the style of his questioning, which more often than not just was Andy rambling on making statements, rather than trying to elicit any meaningful information.

Since Judge Birss had not been provided with the relevant documents in a timely manner the case could not be concluded and therefore ended without a final judgement having been made at the hearing. The judge would need to read the relevant documents before he could give us a decision in writing.

Fortunately, we didn't have long to wait for the verdict. A few days later I got a call from our lawyer Alex Smith to say that we'd won and that Andy had been served with an injunction, stopping him from disseminating his screenplay.

It was such a relief to know that all our efforts had not been in vain.

Andy spoke about contesting the verdict and refused to pay the court costs; Alex eventually engaged the services of a bailiff to collect the debt and this had the desired effect.

Having claimed to be almost penniless he miraculously managed to secure a five-figure sum to settle the case once and for all.

Although Ben and I were both out of pocket at the end of this process, it was vital that we took the action that we did otherwise the film project would have been dead in the water.

This left us even more determined to succeed, and with this in mind, we set up our own production company – PIMM Productions Ltd – in order to get the film made ourselves.

Ben and I, with input from another person, would be responsible for writing the script and Ian would take care of the administration.

You may recall that we first met Andy at a meal at Darlington Football Club. Luckily for us, also present that day was an actor named Bill Fellows; Bill has been in numerous TV programmes and films. As I write this, he is currently starring in *Coronation Street*, where he is playing the character Stu Carpenter.

Anyway, Ian had kept in touch with him since then and asked him if we could meet up to discuss our options.

So, in July 2010 Ian and I met him in a Yarm pub. Following that meeting, Bill agreed to be our advisor and suggested that we meet Sam Claypole, a casting director who had contacts, one of whom could be a director.

The meeting with Sam went ahead. She said she loved the story and wanted to do all she could to help. It was then that we came up with the idea of shooting a trailer. But to do this we needed a director.

A few days after the meeting, Sam emailed me with a possible person for that role, Hartlepool-born Dan Perry. We also had another candidate, who Bill had recommended whose name is lost in the mists of time.

Ian and I together with Sam conducted the interviews in the spare room of a town centre pub.

Straight away when Dan appeared I knew he was our man. I simply loved his enthusiasm. The other guy needn't have turned up!

So now we had a team in place: Bill as advisor, Sam as casting director and Dan as director. Quite an achievement considering the point we had started from.

By this time (December 2010) the first draft of the script was completed. The three of us then set about writing the trailer script.

We agreed to shoot the trailer over two weekends in April 2011. We sourced locations, namely Crook Town Football Club; the Railway Tavern pub in Darlington; Ray Morrison, a former neighbour in Dundee Street, allowed us to use his backyard; the local shop near where I live was also used, as well as my flat!

Sam got several TV actors to play the roles: Bill played my dad, Mark Stobbart (*Auf Wiedersehen, Pet*) played me, Tracy Wilkinson (*Bad Girls*) played my mother, Jamie Baxter (*Emmerdale*, *Still Open All Hours* and *Joe Maddison's War*) played Ian, and finally Sarah Gooch (*Byker Grove*) played Jane.

The four of us financed the trailer, but lots of people helped us out. In addition, Dan, his crew, Sam, Claire Wilkinson (hair), Kelly Kilburn (make-up) and the actors all worked on deferred payment contracts; in layman's terms they would be paid should the feature ever be made and they agreed to appear in it.

The Welling scene, where Darlington clinched promotion back to the Football League in 1990, went well; one slight fly in the ointment was we didn't have quite enough extras.

On the positive side my contact with both former and current Darlington players paid off with Michael Smith, Dan Riley, Adam Reed, Mark Barnard, Neil Wainwright, Mark Forster, together with Ian's brother Graeme, taking part.

One word regarding Michael Smith: this guy is the inspiration I have to succeed in life. When he was 16, like me, Michael was struck down with meningitis. He missed over half his YTS at Darlington because of it, but he fought back to earn himself a professional contract and at the time of writing he was plying his trade for Sheffield Wednesday in the Championship.

This is a fantastic testament to his hard work and determination to succeed in professional football.

One final note regarding Michael, I've followed his career very closely and I am still in touch with him to this day, which is great.

The shoot went far better than we could ever have imagined. Mark played me brilliantly; he got me off to a tee. However, every actor played their own particular part to the best of their ability, which was all we could ask for.

Little did I know then that it would be a further eight years before we would actually start shooting the film.

After our various trips to Cannes and other festivals, the advice that we regularly received was that we needed a more high-profile director attached to our film so that we could secure funding.

In 2013, as I've mentioned earlier in this book, Ian and I co-wrote *An Unfortunate Woman*. After initially agreeing to take on the role of director, Dan had second thoughts and unfortunately dropped out. After doing a lot of research, we secured Sean Cronin, who had previously been in *The Mummy* and involved with the James Bond franchise. Sean actually did a very good job and the film ended up doing really well.

As we looked into the prospect of securing funding for the film, it became dependent on Sean being the director of *Give Them Wings*, so we, as a board, had to make an important and indeed very difficult decision.

Despite having the utmost respect for Dan who had done a brilliant job with the trailer, we unanimously decided to offer the director's role to Sean, who gladly accepted.

However, at the time, this meant Dan still being attached to the project as first assistant director which was a satisfactory outcome since we never wanted to lose his valuable contribution.

At the end of 2015 Ben ended up taking a back seat within PIMM Productions Ltd, and Ian and I bought the other director out of the company. This meant that Ian and I were the two people who had the responsibility of pushing the project forward.

In 2018 Ben actually left the company but remained a shareholder in the film. These changes meant I took on the responsibility of rewriting the script, with Sean's and our executive producer and well-known songwriter Tony Waddington's input; it's something that I really enjoyed doing.

I ended up almost rewriting the whole script, and it was brilliant to be able to put my own ideas to paper, rather than having to take other people's opinions into account. For the first time, since embarking on the project, I was actually 100 per cent happy with the end product.

At around this time Ian and I dispensed with PIMM Productions Ltd, as I'd managed to secure Enterprise Investment Scheme status for our other company, Give Them Wings Productions Ltd, which meant that any UK-based investors could claim tax incentives on their investments from HMRC.

This was a huge step forward for *Give Them Wings*, as you have to jump through hoops for HMRC to obtain this status. In addition, it is a huge incentive when trying to obtain investment.

It was at this time that I became the majority shareholder of GTW Productions Ltd, with Ian and Sean becoming minority shareholders (Sean later gave up his shares). Ben also retained his stake, but isn't a director of the company.

In 2019 Ian, Sean and I managed to raise the funds to shoot *Give Them Wings*. Both Ian and I invested several thousand pounds of our own money, as did our long-term friends David Robinson, Gary Stockill, John Gray and indeed many, many others.

Unfortunately, due to having other commitments at the time of the shoot, Dan couldn't be involved, which looking back was a real shame.

We were absolutely delighted to secure the services of well-known singer and actress Toyah Willcox to play the role of my mother, and Bill Fellows retained the part of my father.

We had to replace Mark Stobbart and James Baxter (neither of whom were available) with newcomer Daniel Watson (who played me) and former *Coronation Street* actor Jacob Anderton, who took on the role of Ian. Both were brilliant; Daniel in particular excelled in his role.

The only disappointing thing for me was the fact that due to ongoing health issues, I couldn't go on the set as much as I would have liked. This was a real shame, looking back now.

The film was released to much acclaim in July 2022 in the UK. We had premieres in Darlington and London, both of which went down really well. As I sit here typing this today, we have a really good sales agent on board called Michael Cowan. To date, we have distribution deals in the UK, Latin America, Scandinavia and Australia and New Zealand. Others are in the pipeline for the USA and Europe.

It wasn't all plain sailing. A lot of people in the film business aren't what they seem and Ian and I have certainly learned some lessons; ones that will be invaluable should we decide to make another film.

One final comment: Ian stood by me for the whole time we were fighting to make what was a dream become a reality. I shall be for ever grateful to him for that.

On a separate note since retiring from work, I've had two books published: *Give Them Wings* and *100 of the Best*. *Give Them Wings* was an update of *Flipper's Side*, which was published in 2000, and *100 of the Best* is about my favourite 100 games I've witnessed while supporting my beloved Darlington FC. Both have sold really well, which I'm very pleased about.

Continuing with the writing theme, I have also written three scripts: *The Hill*, *John's Journey* and *Give*

Them Wings 2. All three have won writing awards (at the time of writing, I have won more than 40 in total); this is something that I'm extremely proud of. I'm also a producer for a film called *Solid Venom* with a very good friend of mine called Matt Bland, who incidentally worked with me on both *An Unfortunate Woman* and *Give Them Wings*. All being well, we hope to shoot this in 2024 or 2025. So, as you will appreciate, I have a lot going on.

Looking back over my life, I think I've achieved everything I set out to do, despite quite a lot of bumps along the way.

I have a brilliant, supportive wife, who backs me in whatever I want to do, which is all that I could ask for.

The small band of ever-loyal friends – Ian Carter, Stephen Lowson, John Gray, Gary Stockill, Mark Forster, Matt Bland and Dale Anderson – are absolutely fantastic and I'm extremely grateful for the help and support they have given me over the years.

I feel that I must also mention Darlington FC CEO David Johnston, who, over the past 18 months, has become a good friend and has supported me a lot.

Finally, my last comment has to be about my mother. As you will realise by now, she always taught me to be as independent as I can. I'm really glad she was like that, because it made me the man I am today! I honestly think that if she was here today, she'd be super proud of what I've achieved. I certainly hope so anyway.